SINGAPORE

MELBOURNE

RIO DE JANEIRO

BANGKOK

COTTESLOE

NEW YORK

PERTH

LOS ANGELES

50 OF THE WORLD'S BEST APARTMENTS

50 OF THE WORLD'S BEST APARTMENTS

Published in Australia in 2004 by
The Images Publishing Group Pty Ltd
ABN 89 059 734 431
6 Bastow Place, Mulgrave, Victoria, 3170, Australia
Telephone: +61 3 9561 5544 Facsimile: +61 3 9561 4860
Email: books@images.com.au
Website: www.imagespublishinggroup.com

National Library of Australia
Cataloguing-in-Publication entry:

50 of the world's best apartments.

Includes index.
ISBN 1 920744 49 5.

1. Apartments. 2. Interior architecture. I. Title: Fifty of the world's best apartments.

643.27

Coordinating Editor: Robyn Beaver

Designed by The Graphic Image Studio Pty Ltd, Mulgrave, Australia
Website: www.tgis.com.au

Film by Mission Productions Limited, Hong Kong
Printed by Everbest Printing Co. Ltd. in Hong Kong/China

CONTENTS

50 OF THE WORLD'S BEST APARTMENTS

Fifty

50

13TH STREET RESIDENCE   NEW YORK, NEW YORK, USA   MARBLE FAIRBANKS ARCHITECTS

The client, previously an art director, is a collector of American folk art. The program was to incorporate his art collection into the design of this one-bedroom, 1800-square-foot, second-floor loft. A range of materials was used to set up episodic scenes to both frame the art and choreograph movement through the space. The ceiling height allowed the architects to insert a library mezzanine with suspended steel shelves and a minimal steel walkway that bridges the space, dividing more public living from the private bedroom/dressing/bathroom suite.

Material transparency, reflectivity, and a variety of textured opacities expand and reconfigure spatial relationships. The material palette includes blackened hot-rolled steel plates, etched glass, dyed fiber board, poured-in-place concrete, ebonized cherry and plaster for wall surfaces, and slate, limestone and oak for floor surfaces.

1   View toward kitchen and entry from library wall
2   Dining and living room

1

2

3

4

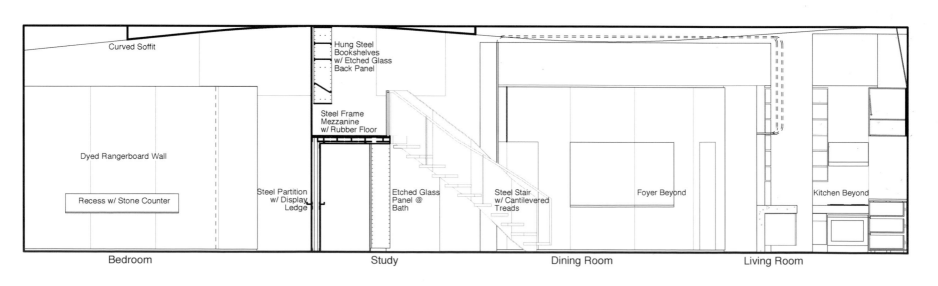

5

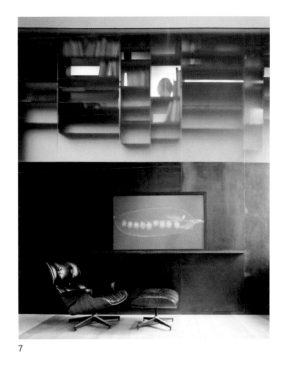

7

9

10

8 Library wall and mezzanine with bathroom display niches above

9 Kitchen

10 View of entry and ebonized cherry display wrapper from living room

11

12

13

14

11   Guest bathroom
12   Bedroom, dressing room, and bathroom
13   Bedroom and mezzanine overlook
14   Living room and dining room from entry

Photography: Gregory Goode Photography

A PLACE IN THE SUN   RIO DE JANEIRO, BRAZIL   ANDRÉ PIVA ARQUITETURA

For his own apartment, architect André Piva has used a restrained design strategy to create an ethereal 'vacation' environment. The fantastic view of Rio creates a vivid counterpoint to the neutral palette.

For the architect the most important design factor, excluding the external environment, was the concept of a loft. The three-level, 500-square-meter apartment is located in the heart of Rio, in the Rodrigo de Freitas' lagoon. The first floor accommodates the master bedroom and the guest room. The second floor is the living area, with the living, dining, and the American kitchen, in one area. The spectacular terrace, complete with swimming pool and views of Corcovado and the statue of Christ, is also on the second floor. The service area, family room and library are on the third-floor mezzanine.

The stripped-back, clean design with its white walls and limestone floors, deliberately eliminated extraneous features. White aluminum and brushed steel contribute to the minimalist color palette of white, off-white and black.

1 Living room staircase with guardrail in brushed steel balances limestone floor

2   Double-height living area is linked to mezzanine; couch and wood furniture designed by architect
3   Second floor plan
4   First floor plan

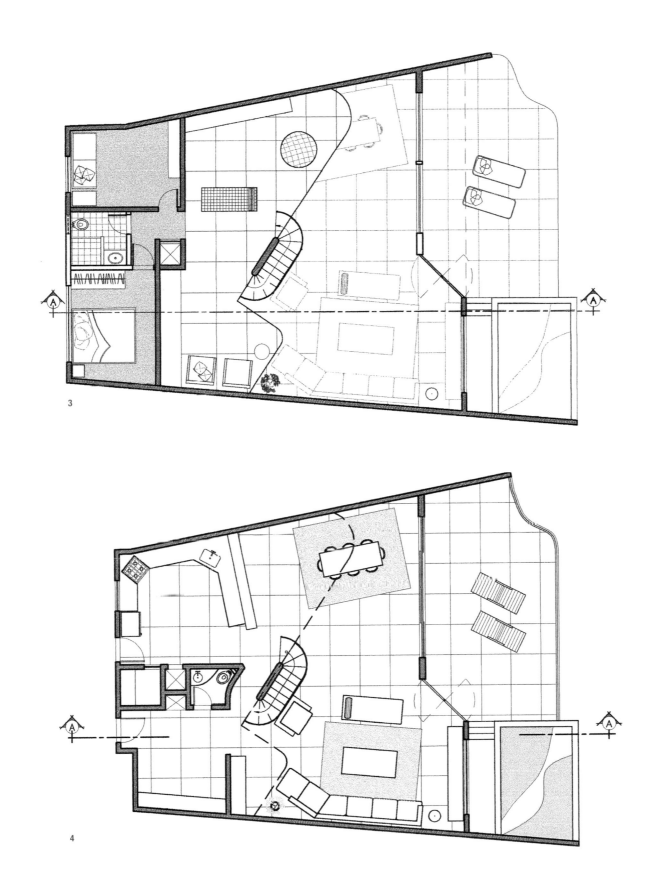

3

4

5

6

7

5 Suspended swimming pool has Corcovado and the statue of Christ as its backdrop

6 Mezzanine view of dining room and city view beyond

7 Master bathroom detail

Opposite
Terrace, with superb view of Rio, has limestone floor

Photography: Jayme Acioli

APARTMENT 15, AKM BUILDING   MELBOURNE, VICTORIA, AUSTRALIA

JACKSON CLEMENTS BURROWS ARCHITECTS

Apartment 15 is located on the top floor of the AKM building, one of a small group of significant brick warehouses that formerly housed a range of textile-related industries.

The 210-square-meter apartment is divided into two main volumes spread over four levels. A fifth level accommodates a 40-square-meter roof deck, boasting uninterrupted views of the city skyline and surrounding parklands.

The first two levels sit within the existing glazed sawtooth roof and benefit from extensive natural lighting. The lower (entry) level accommodates an open plan living area and linear strip kitchen. The next level houses a study/bedroom and a generous bathroom contains an inset bath set against a glazed truss; stainless steel benches respond to the industrial heritage of the original building.

Continuing upstairs, one leaves the first volume and passes out of the main building into the second volume housed on the bridge structure over the laneway. This space within the original bridge structure accommodates the master bedroom and an additional bedroom fronting the south side.

Polished black butt stairs lead to the retreat lounge on the fourth level. The entire western wall is glazed with sliding door panels that retract to a cantilevered position beyond the walls overhanging the laneway below. Solar gain from this west-facing retractable glazed wall was a concern and a series of external, computer-controlled retractable aluminium louvers were installed to address this issue. Further sensors assess wind loads and retract the aluminium louvers when wind speeds are excessive, protecting the system from damage.

A further stair extends upward. Rising from a series of layered timber platforms, the stair arrives at a precarious landing hovering in front of a blue glazed, 5-meter corner window. The unnerving view down into the laneway some 20 meters below is only relieved by the expansive roof deck which unfolds to uninterrupted views in all directions.

1   View to Melbourne city skyline from retreat living space

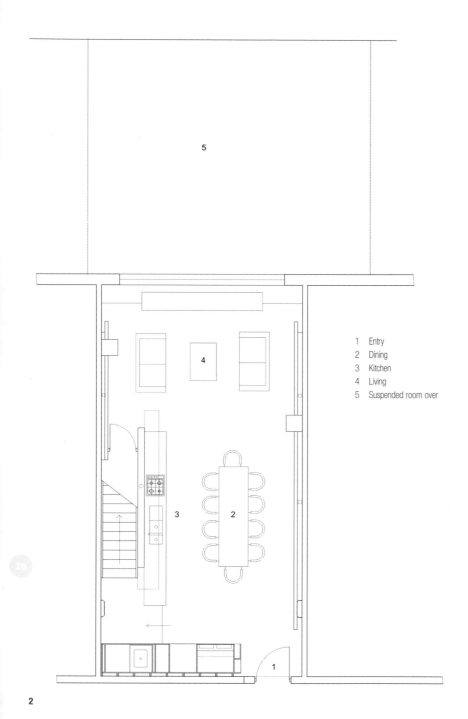

1 Entry
2 Dining
3 Kitchen
4 Living
5 Suspended room over

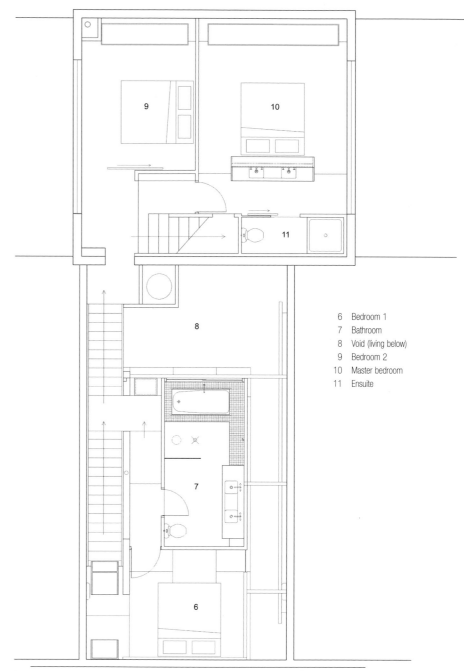

6   Bedroom 1
7   Bathroom
8   Void (living below)
9   Bedroom 2
10 Master bedroom
11 Ensuite

2

3

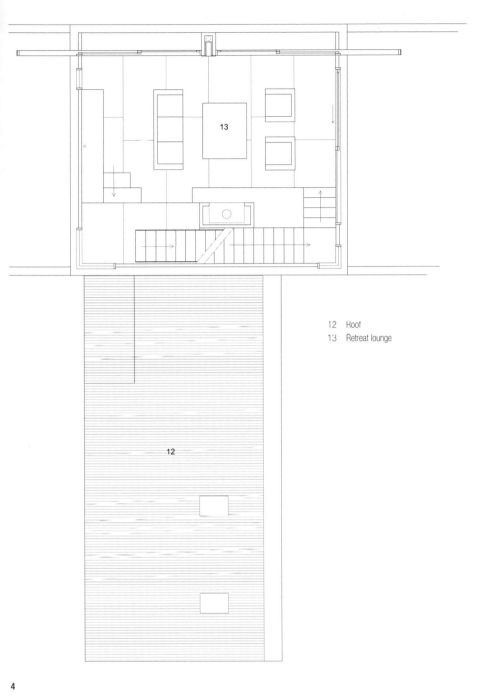

12 Roof
13 Retreat lounge

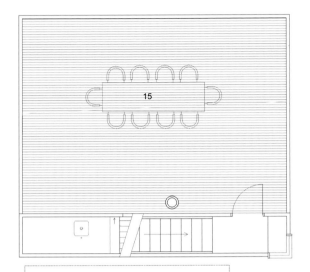

14 Roof below
15 Roof deck

4

5

2 Ground floor plan
3 Mezzanine/Level 2 plan
4 Level 3 plan
5 Roof plan

7

9

10

8

Opposite

    Entry level living space

7   Integrated kitchen and laundry at entry level

8   Mezzanine bathroom under sawtooth

9   View of Melbourne city from roof deck

10   Cantilevered doors reveal retreat living space

11 Master bedroom with integrated ensuite
12 Integrated ensuite to master bedroom

Photography: Trevor Mein

11

12

APARTMENT AT SAILENDRA   JAKARTA, INDONESIA   PAI — PARAMITA ABIRAMA ISTASADHYA, PT

Located in the central business district of Jakarta, on the 18th floor of the JW Marriott Hotel tower, this apartment is elegantly furnished with high-quality furniture, fabrics, and the owner's own collection of artworks. Most of the interior architectural elements, including the ceilings, doors and walls, were renovated or relocated in the architect's new design for the apartment. The color scheme is light and neutral, with deep wood accents, creating a modern and restful ambience.

1   Living room, dining room and study
2   Main living room facing the foyer

2

1

3 Dining room
4 Master bedroom
5 Study
6 Master bathroom
7 Floor plan

Photography: Iskandar Irawan

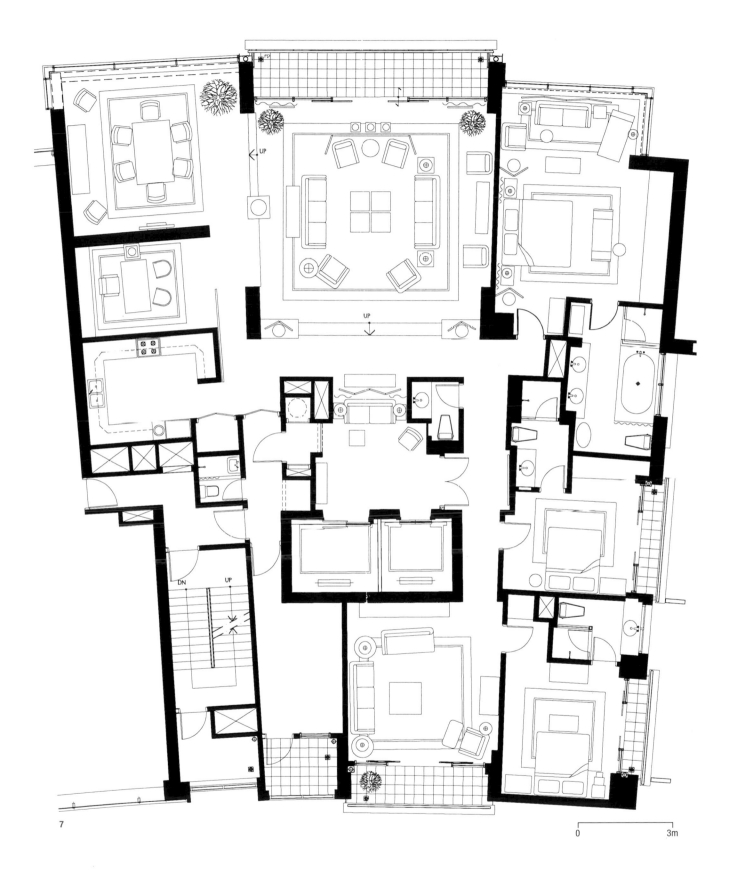

7

0 3m

APARTMENT AT THANA CITY   BANGKOK, THAILAND   DWP CL3

Located on the 15th and 16th floors of a residential building on the outskirts of Bangkok, this 700-square-meter apartment enjoys panoramic views of the surrounding rural landscape and an abundance of natural light. With these elements as the primary focus and inspiration for the design concept, the brief was to create a relaxing family environment and an elegant venue for evening entertaining. The apartment would also be a showcase for the owner's vast collection of antique Asian furniture and artworks. The intention was that the pieces would be integrated into the design and work as part of it rather than be placed after completion. The simplicity and clarity of the architecture was therefore of paramount importance.

The existing interior was completely refurbished to create five ensuite bedrooms and a variety of formal and informal living spaces. Entry to the apartment is through an oversize pivot-hinged timber door, which opens to a large, bright entrance hallway. A timber portal marks the transition from the foyer to the living spaces while a narrow corridor leads to the kitchen and utility areas. A curved staircase leads to the second floor and a comfortable family room. This room features a mini bar with mirror-faced cabinets and an entertainment center concealed behind a sliding timber panel. The bedrooms are accessed from this space. Full-height curved windows stretch over both floors and allow light to flood the space during the day. A library was built in the double-height stairwell left by a demolished staircase.

The apartment strikes a balance between design and comfort, form and function, while being influenced by both contemporary minimalism and traditional Asian architectural forms. A restricted palette of materials was used with key finishes such as dark timber, sandstone and limestone, selected for their relevance to both traditional Asian architecture and contemporary minimal interiors.

1   Master bedroom. The ensuite is behind the etched glass wall.

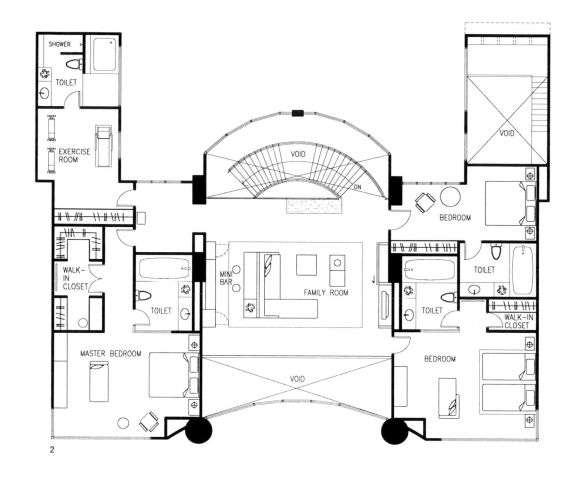

SHOWER
TOILET
EXERCISE ROOM
VOID
VOID
BEDROOM
WALK-IN CLOSET
TOILET
MINI BAR
FAMILY ROOM
TOILET
TOILET
WALK-IN CLOSET
MASTER BEDROOM
DN
VOID
BEDROOM

2

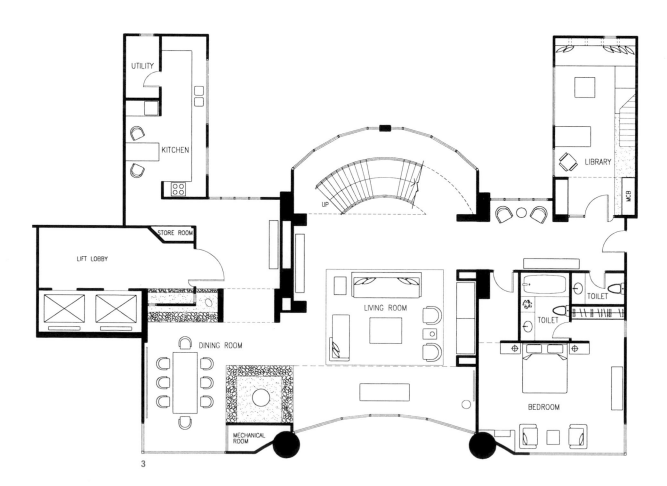

UTILITY
KITCHEN
LIBRARY
STORE ROOM
LIFT LOBBY
MCB
UP
TOILET
TOILET
DINING ROOM
LIVING ROOM
MECHANICAL ROOM
BEDROOM

3

5

4

6

7

2 Upper floor plan
3 Lower floor plan
4 View from living area up to mezzanine floor
5 Library
6 Living area with selection of artworks
7 Detail of library stair

9

10

8   Curved staircase leading to mezzanine floor
9   Kitchen
10 View through to dining area

11

12

13

11 Living area

12 Entry is through an oversized pivot-hinged timber door

13 Buddha hand on raised sandstone platform surrounded by pebble bed

14 Exterior of the apartment showing terrace decking

Photography: Eddie Siu

APARTMENT FOR AN AUTHOR NEW YORK, NEW YORK, USA CENTERBROOK ARCHITECTS AND PLANNERS

This is the renovation of a foyer, dining room, and library/writing studio in a New York duplex apartment. The client, a noted author, wanted it to be elegant, yet comfortable and efficient for her daily chore of putting words to paper. She also desired a work of invention, superior craftsmanship, and lasting value.

Sitting below the upper penthouse floor, which is glassy and light, the renovation offers a counterpoint—a vaulted retreat—a place to dine on cold winter nights and to work year-round, hidden away from the world.

Working within a shell of uninspired gypsum board box spaces, new ceilings, cabinets, and columns were created from teak, rendered in an invented classic style. Teak is easy to work with, allowing high relief. While it appears warm, the coloration has a slight green cast that accentuates its modeling and the craft of the cabinetmaker. A deep terra cotta red was chosen as the color behind the walls as a contrast to the teak; lighting is hidden in the column capitals to further give the ceilings a soft glow at night.

Desks and bookshelves were designed with great care, offering 'a place for everything and everything in its place.' Some drawers are shallow with felt liners and folding metal rods that hold down loose stacks of typed pages. These allow the writer to have readily available book chapters in semi-disarray and yet be able to 'close up shop' at a moment's notice.

In the middle of the three spaces is a staircase with art nouveau-like wrought iron railings leading up to the penthouse. A few shallow steps at the window end of the library lead up to a raised platform with a view of Central Park beyond.

The final result of all this effort is an apartment with a strong sense of itself. Designed to withstand the whims of an inveterate collector, it still has enough character to meld eclectic origins and become a remarkable place of its own.

Opposite
Study

2

3

2 Entry
3 Dining room
4 Lower level floor plan

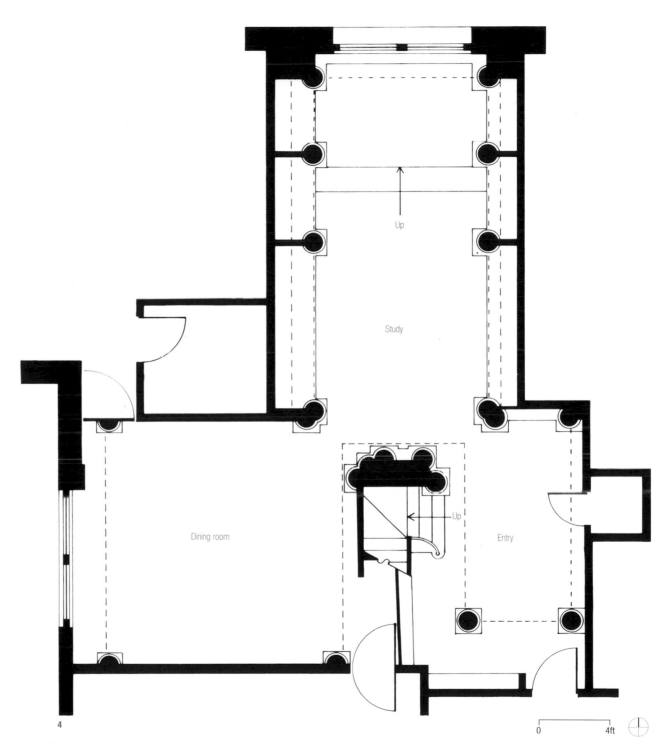

Study

Dining room

Up

Up

Entry

4

0   4ft

5

6

5 Study
6 Desk detail
7 Stair to upper penthouse level
Photography: Timothy Hursley

APARTMENT IN SÃO PAULO   SÃO PAULO, BRAZIL   CAROLINA SZABÓ INTERIORS

From afar, everything looks normal, very urban. An apartment like thousands of others, surrounded by concrete, glass, wood, a little green, a little cloud, a little sun. A lot of São Paulo city. Up close, the 370-square-meter apartment has the stiff contemporary demeanor one expects, yet the landscape disturbs. The hills of the concrete city are just an entrée to what lies inside closed doors.

In this cozy contemporary apartment, Carolina Szabó, a highly honored interior architect and president for many years of the ABD (Brazilian Designers Association) who has lived in São Paulo city all her life, has translated into walls and furnishings what she believes an interior decoration should be: a contemporary space, very comfortable, easy and surrounded by superb Brazilian art and crafts.

Carolina transformed this apartment twice; the first time for a couple and their children and the second time for the couple themselves. When the children left home, the walls of their rooms were removed, forming a spacious bedroom with a sitting room. The balcony was turned into a small and charming atelier for the owner's painting.

The main goal was to design an integrated ambience. From inside one can see the concrete city but far from being cold, this apartment emerges as a fabulous and relaxed place in which to live.

1 Living room detail

2

3

4

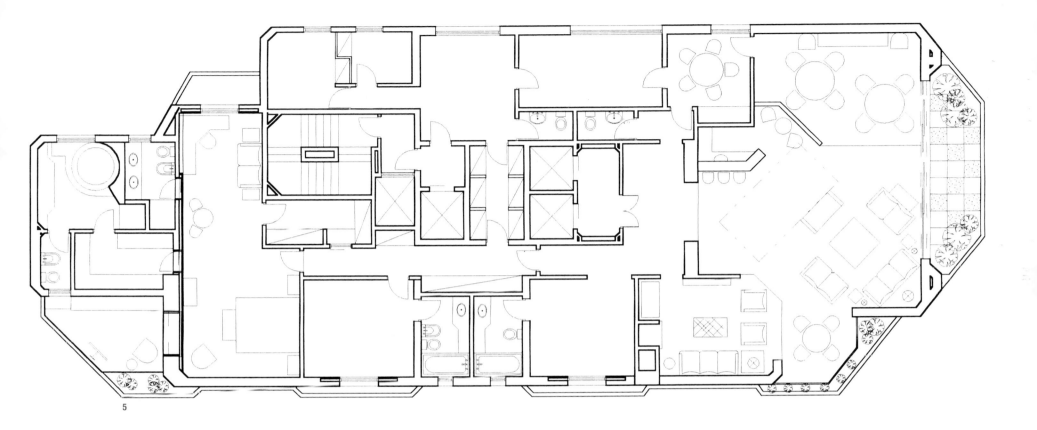

5

6

2 Main view from the living room and dining room
3 Living room detail
4 Living room
5 Floor plan
6 TV room

7

8

9

10

11

12

13

APARTMENT ON CENTRAL PARK WEST NEW YORK, NEW YORK, USA LEROY STREET STUDIO

Two classic pre-war apartments were combined to create a single 7200-square-foot unit for an artist couple and their three children. The clients were interested in the juxtaposition of unusual materials and forms. The two units were very cellular, and had an unusually deep floor plate; the architects introduced a court, detailed as an external space, as a central hub of the apartment to make it feel more open. The court's massive plaster walls were carved to create recessed bench seating, and back-lit niches with embedded antique Philippine shell screens. Japanese paper streamers weave across the ceiling between wire tension cables.

Off this main court is a corrugated steel grain silo which contains a plywood-lined dining room with a ceiling of tensile fabric. An 11-foot steel, pine and fiberglass sliding door separates the main court from the kitchen with its translucent plastic and aluminum cabinetry and 4-inch-thick cherry butcher block counters. Beyond the living room a steel and wood screen defines a broad arc dividing the master bedroom into a sitting area with cast colored glass fiber-optic lights embedded in a stained concrete slab, and a sleeping area on a raised platform with a ceiling carved with a pattern of protozoan lights. The children's playroom sits off the master bedroom with undulating astro-turf and recessed golf holes, wrap-around panoramic views of golf courses, and amoebic-shaped recessed lights.

1 View from master bedroom suite sitting area toward bedroom

1 Master suite
2 Bedroom
3 Playroom
4 Kitchen
5 Central court
6 Dining drum
7 Living room
8 A/V room
9 Entry/powder room

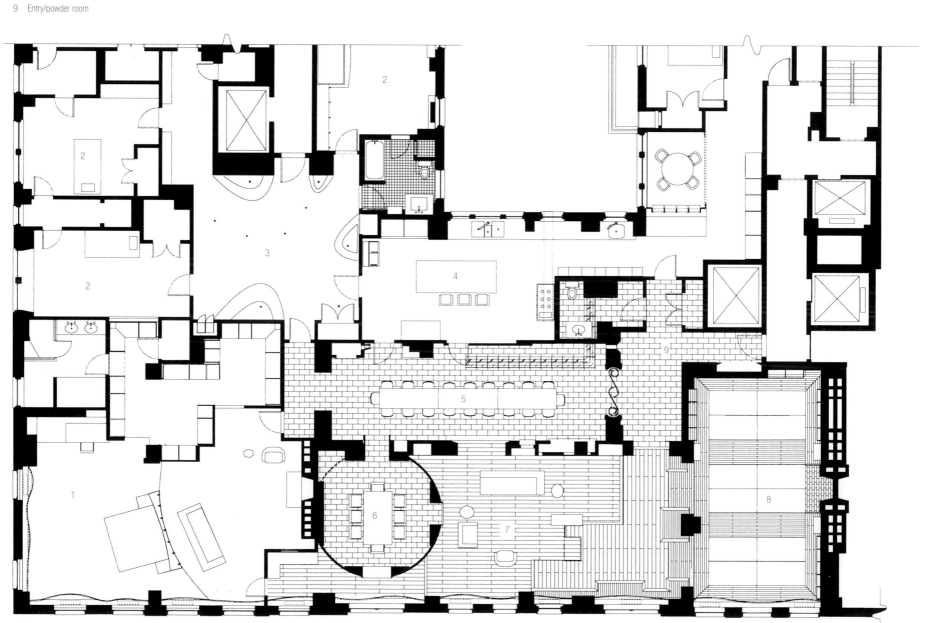

2

4

3

5

6

7

8

6   View from entry foyer into central court

7   View from living room through central court to kitchen

8   Dining drum has views to Central Park

9   View from master bedroom suite sleeping area toward sitting area

10 Powder room at front foyer

Photography: Michael Kleinberg

10

9

AQUILON APARTMENTS   SYDNEY, NEW SOUTH WALES, AUSTRALIA   DEM (AUST) PTY LTD

Aquilon and the Terraces is a combined development of 139 apartments and 13 terraces. A feature concept of the development is the high residential amenity achieved with use of private outdoor, open space in a 'loggia' or 'indoor/outdoor room' allowing the flexible flow of floor space and maximizing the space amenity of the dwellings. This is expanded where possible with corner units, which have kitchens that extend into the loggia for outdoor barbeque and entertainment.

The loggia has a 'permeable' external façade skin of glass and timber louvers which are individually adjustable and operable so that maximum flexibility can be achieved in response to privacy, sun and wind protection, and enclosure.

Internal planning provides for a number of unit and amenity types: double-story ground and penthouses, and standard single-sided and corner units in various sizes. The apartments are designed for flexibility, space and light. Plans promote multi-tasking of space: corner units have a second-bedroom bi-fold door extension from the living room, and 'structureless' glass sliding corners where the doors open to create 'open' corners. The living zone can be greatly expanded as needed and is larger than expected for typical two-bedroom apartments. Glazing is generally floor-to-ceiling onto ledges, which further expands the apparent space. The main ensuite bathroom has a glazed wall borrowing natural light from the bedroom. Where there are longer internal corridors the walls have been warped to 'disfigure' the long space and create entry statements for each unit.

Most of the energy performance of the building is achieved by passive means. North, east and the exposed corner of the west elevation are protected by the external skin of the loggia/louver systems. Other floor-to-ceiling windows are recessed and protected by large overhangs. The building materials were, where possible, considered for environmental impact and this partly drove the decision to use a renewable timber louver shutter system rather than the high embodied energy full aluminum system.

1   Penthouse courtyard
2   Loggia seen from living room
3   Penthouse loggia

1

3

2

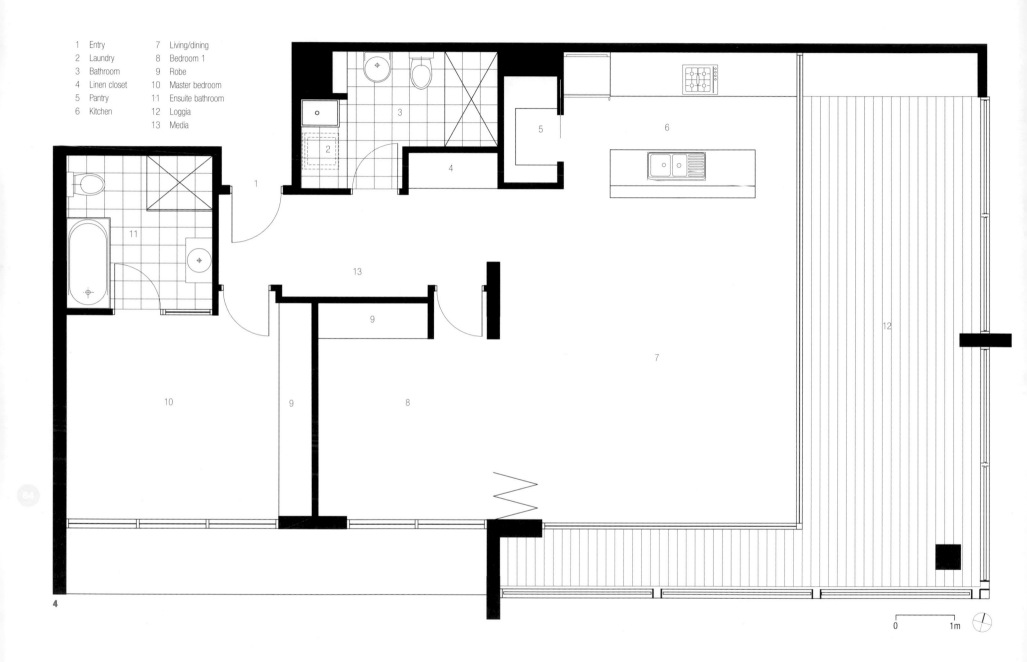

1   Entry
2   Laundry
3   Bathroom
4   Linen closet
5   Pantry
6   Kitchen
7   Living/dining
8   Bedroom 1
9   Robe
10 Master bedroom
11 Ensuite bathroom
12 Loggia
13 Media

0   1m

4   Floor plan
5   Living room and loggia
6   Penthouse kitchen
7   Kitchen
8   Penthouse interior and loggia
9   Penthouse opens to outdoors

5

7

8

6

9

10

11

12

10   Penthouse courtyard
11   Penthouse bedroom
12   Second bedroom
13   Penthouse bathroom

Photography: Martin van der Wal, courtesy of Sterling Estates

CAIRNHILL PLAZA APARTMENT SINGAPORE SCDA ARCHITECTS

This 2300-square-foot apartment is located on the fifth floor of a residential building. The renovation included the conversion of an existing bedroom into a family/media room area with a large sandblasted glass sliding door that had to be transported into the apartment by crane, as it was too large for the elevator. A water feature and reflecting pool were incorporated into the terrace, adding a peaceful aspect to the treetop views beyond. The kitchen renovation is modern, with extensive use of stainless steel and black granite for the cabinets, counter tops and appliances.

Other materials used in the renovation include beige limestone internal flooring, white volax marble in the bathrooms, teak wood as a feature in the bedroom, and bush hammer rustic white granite for external flooring.

1 Terra cotta urn from Chengmai acts as a focal point for living room

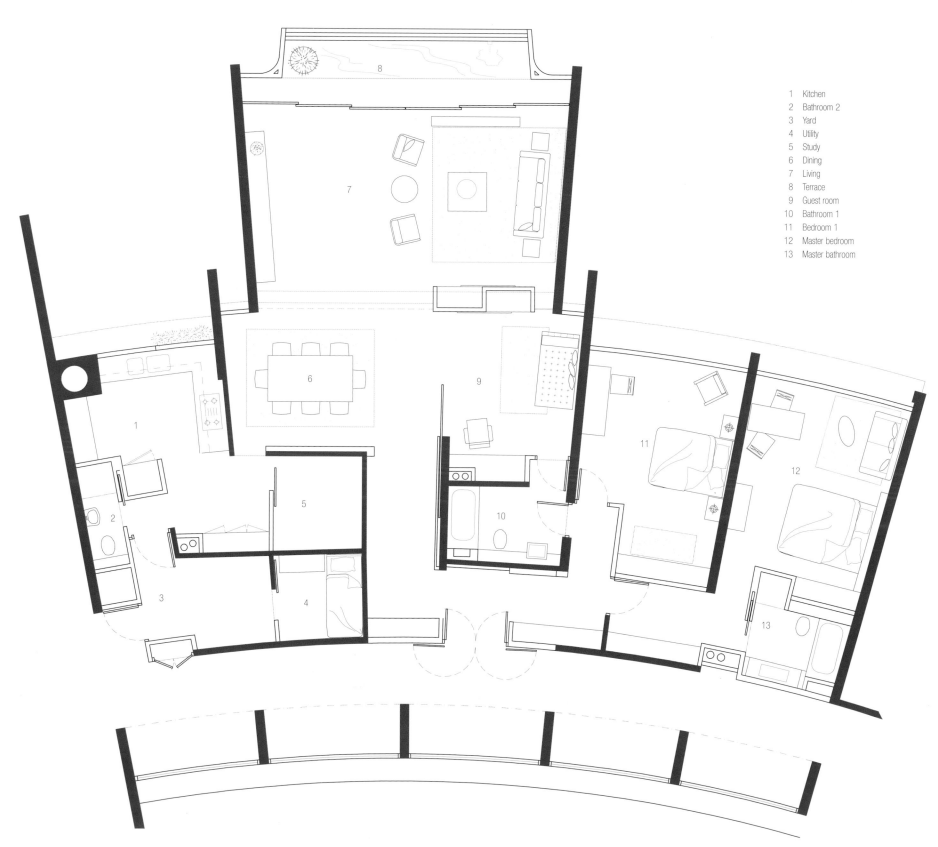

1   Kitchen
2   Bathroom 2
3   Yard
4   Utility
5   Study
6   Dining
7   Living
8   Terrace
9   Guest room
10 Bathroom 1
11 Bedroom 1
12 Master bedroom
13 Master bathroom

4

5

4 View of dining area
5 Balcony area filled with water acts as a reflective pool
6 Detail of door pull
7 Detail of timber slate front door with sandblasted glass between
8 White volax marble lines interior of the master bathroom

Photography: Ken Seet/SCDA Architects

6

7

CENTRAL PARK WEST RESIDENCE   NEW YORK, NEW YORK, USA   JANSON GOLDSTEIN LLP

The apartment was designed to display the owner's collections of art, furniture and objects. With expansive views of New York's Central Park, the project is a home for living, viewing and exploring the many things within it.

In the 'public' areas a terrazzo floor flows from the entry, into the living area and dining, providing a gallery quality to the space. The ceiling plane is manipulated to have a sculpted presence with recessed lighting located for specific art pieces on the walls. HVAC and window treatments are integrated into the ceiling design.

For the 'private' areas (master suite, library, guest room, bath) a bleached wood floor is used. At the bed the wood turns up the wall into a suede headboard which provides both comfort and a reference line for the Utta Barth photographs which hang above. Cantilevered steel side tables complete the composition. Bath areas have a serene feel with limestone floors and teak wood with an oil finish. Plaster walls, which match the limestone floor, add to the texture of the space and counterbalance the cool white mosaic marble and white Corian counter tops.

The interior design is a blend of mid-century design with pieces by Jean Nouvel (dining room table), Alison Berger (hand blown floor lamp) and custom pieces by Janson Goldstein (onyx table, dining room banquette). The collection of photography includes work by Richard Avedon, Sally Mann and Utta Barth. A James Turrell hologram sits at the entry. Italian glass work, African masks, an original Olivetti typewriter, and handsewn quilts are some of the objects.

1   View into bedroom/study

1 Entry
2 Living
3 Dining
4 Master suite
5 Master bath
6 Guest bath
7 Guest room
8 Kitchen

7

6

8

3

1

CLOSET

Storage

5

2

CLOSET

6

4

N.I.C.

REF

DOUBLE
OVEN

Lamp

Lamp

3

4

5

2 Floor plan
3 View from dining into living room
4 View toward entry
5 View toward entry; James Turrell hologram in background

6 View at entry; living area beyond

7 Study with original Olivetti typewriter in foreground, custom-designed desk by Janson Goldstein in background

8 View into dining area and Richard Avedon photos; Joan Nouvel table with custom-designed banquette by Janson Goldstein

9 View into kitchen; polished white cabinets with stainless steel and skylight

7

6

8

10

11

10   Bed detail with wood floor meeting suede headboard, Utta Barth photos above with cantilevered custom-designed metal side tables by Janson Goldstein

11   Master bath with teak wood, limestone floor, white mosaic walls, and custom Corian counter

Photography: Paul Warchol

CLASSIC DELIGHT   SÃO PAULO, BRAZIL   OSCAR MIKAIL

In Buenos Aires everyone knows La Recoleta, and in Rio de Janeiro, Copacabana and Ipanema are well known, but São Paulo has secrets. Some of the best houses and apartments are hidden away, located in places that make this city one of the most complex in the world. The 'São Paulo-ness' of São Paulo is a fugitive quality, hard to define and even harder to capture in the design of an apartment. Certain moments give the city its special character—the rain that sometimes falls for days on end, or the beautiful sunshine that sparkles its light in the concrete and glass buildings in Paulista Avenue.

The details that arrest the eye often originate in São Paulo shops, that offer everything from modern to classical, from traditional to bizarre. São Paulo interior architects and designers have an advantage because they know all these large and small stores where they can indulge their clients' wishes.

The architect Oscar Mikail has an eclectic taste, which he can indulge on behalf of his clients, in the stores of São Paulo. His goal for this classic home was to make it a city apartment with an urban sophistication. The 500-square-meter apartment in a chic neighborhood features artworks from the 18th and 19th centuries, mixed with contemporary furniture and modern technology. All the interior details such as the marble and wood floor, the lighting, and the plaster framing were designed by the architect.

Opposite
A 19th-century French round table divides the living room

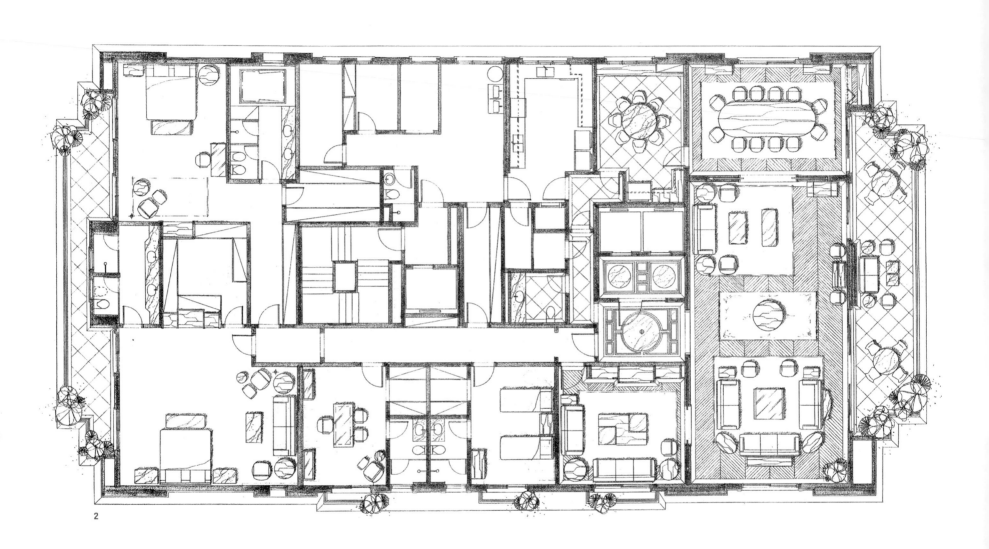

2

3

4

5

6

9

Opposite
His bathroom features Italian marble

8 Her bathroom in elegant Italian marble and light color palette

9 Her master bedroom with feminine chandelier and floral English engravings over the bed

10 His master bedroom mixes modern and traditional elements

Photography: Alain Brugier

8

10

COLOR AND LIGHT   SÃO PAULO, BRAZIL   BRUNETE FRACCAROLI

Color, light, and function are the main characteristics of the work of Brunete Fraccaroli, a leading Brazilian interior designer. This apartment could be in any part of the world but it is located in São Paulo, where the variety of different people and tastes is very influential. The game of light and color and the mixture of materials creates a contemporary language. When one enters the apartment, he or she will never feel lonely or sad. This is the magic that Brunete creates.

The entrance hall, where white Carrara marble meets the light wood floor, is a feature of the architect's repertoire. The owner, a very famous television personality in Brazil, wanted a place where he and his family could rest after a busy day of work. At the same time he also wanted a place where contemporary aspects would be the most important: light rooms that are full of color. The peaceful white color contrasting with the strong orange and red colors of the laminated mirror in the fireplace room is one of the most perfect contrasts in the apartment.

The main design is based on the functional aspects of the spaces and on the contrast between the different colors and materials.

2

4

3

2 Living room with fireplace room in background
3 Fireplace room is a cozy, contemporary room for watching television
4 Living room welcomes family and friends with Italian and Brazilian contemporary furniture
5 Entrance hall with Carrara marble and intriguing painted mural

6

6 Dining room with table designed by the architect in black and white glass

7 Closets feature mirror doors, to contrast with the wooden floor

8 Master bedroom features wall-size photograph of the owners

Photography: Tuca Reines

7

DARLING POINT APARTMENT SYDNEY, NEW SOUTH WALES, AUSTRALIA STANIC HARDING ARCHITECTS

This doughnut shaped, 155-square-meter apartment was stripped back and redesigned to celebrate the potential of an unhindered circular journey. The space was to ooze out to the perimeter while keeping the core unencumbered. A series of sliding doors along the journey pull away from the core into the radiating walls that define individual rooms. Being conscious of the spaces between the ends of these walls and the core, the edges were curved and splayed to counter the regular walnut core paneling. Connecting all these spaces allowed for wonderful vistas to the city skyline, Sydney Harbour or the tree canopies.

The existing entry from the lift lobby led straight into a services cabinet. This was reconfigured to provide a direct connection to the Bay and the external balcony. A bedroom was removed to allow the combined living/dining spaces to enjoy an unencumbered view. The existing services cabinet was clad in a curvaceous metallic silver paneling to create display niches, storage, a fold-down bar and housing for sound equipment. This once unsightly element is now a very useful space-maker, separating the television zone from the general area.

The paneled core is designed to contrast with the glazed perimeter and to ground the occupant. As with previous projects, the core accommodates laundries, robes, and storage that are hidden to the casual visitor. Mirror paneling bends the space, giving glimpses of the view. The scheme celebrates the circle and the edge conditions that result from planning within it.

1   Circular plan offers spectacular connection to Sydney Harbour and Bay

1   Entry
2   Services
3   TV area
4   Kitchen
5   Study 1
6   Bathroom 1
7   Bedroom 1
8   Bedroom/study 2
9   Hall
10 Bathroom 2
11 Living
12 Dining
13 Balcony
14 Fire stair
15 Lift lobby
16 Lift 1
17 Lift 2
18 Laundry
19 Walk-in robe
20 Robe

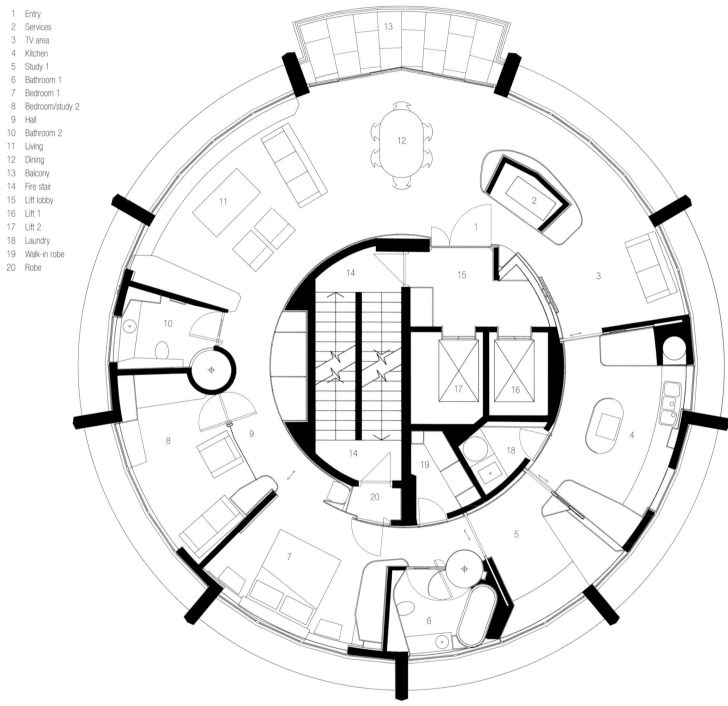

2

3

4

5

2 Circular floor plan

3 Each radiating wall edge is considered as part
   of the journey

4 Detail of high-gloss pod and view to
   dining/balcony

5 Curved paneling and stepped ceiling planes
   celebrate the circular plan

6 Walnut-lined core connecting rooms along the perimeter
7 Curved pod appears to push into ceiling plane
8 Kitchen elements have either curved ends or follow the perimeter

9

10

11

9 Silver pod divides television area from dining/living spaces

10 Sliding door is concealed in kitchen/study joinery wall

11 View between core and room joinery showing round glass shower

12 Colored glass and mirror paneled walls reflect light and view

13 Core 'shifts' in main bedroom to form alcove reflected in door

Photography: Paul Gosney

DOCKLANDS PENTHOUSE MELBOURNE, VICTORIA, AUSTRALIA HPA ARCHITECTS

Melbourne has witnessed significant residential development throughout its extensive Docklands precinct. This building is an urban site defined on the east by the sweeping curve of the Lorimer Street Bridge and west along the axis of Melbourne's remnant infrastructure works. The northern and southern views read tall and slender, gold and sharp.

The penthouse levels are positioned for all to see, in a gold box on top. The floating box sits precariously on the building creating large cantilevers.

Full floor-to-ceiling glass wraps around the apartment's perimeter, maximizing the vantage point and revealing truly breathtaking views. The apartment juts out to allow sweeping views down the Yarra River toward the Bolte Bridge, and across to Melbourne's central business district.

The three-bedroom apartment features an open living zone and linear kitchen. The original third bedroom has since been deleted to allow an expansive living area. The living zones are collected in a single open tube, which opens up to a large outdoor terrace defined by the roof to the levels below. The kitchen is detailed to give a continuation from inside to outside and is located adjacent to the outdoor dining terrace, separated only be a glazed screen. Large sliding walls open to create strong inside–outside connections. Bedrooms are provided with a full external frontage taking advantage of the magnificent views.

1 Living areas
2 Kitchen zone

1

2

3

4

5

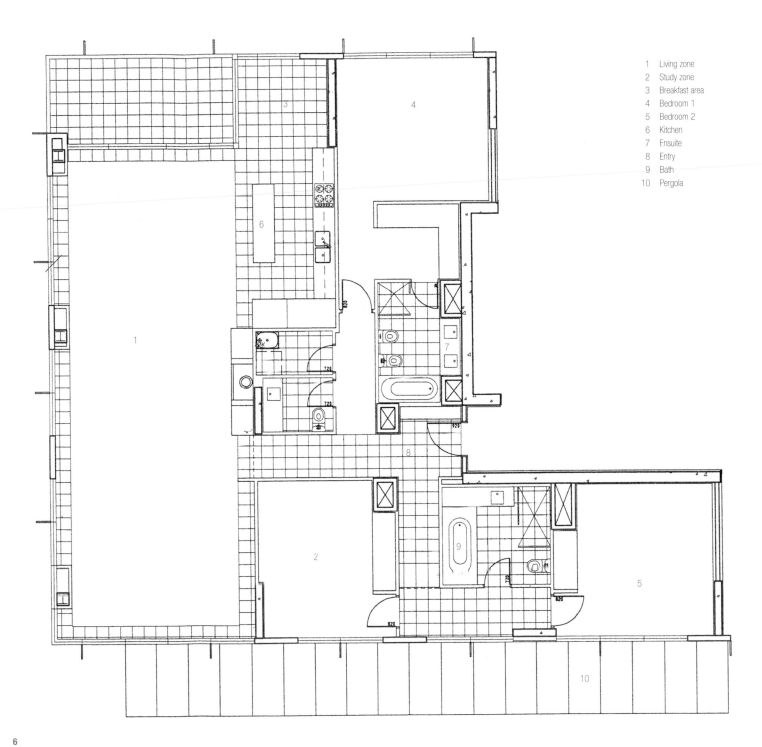

1   Living zone
2   Study zone
3   Breakfast area
4   Bedroom 1
5   Bedroom 2
6   Kitchen
7   Ensuite
8   Entry
9   Bath
10   Pergola

3   Living room
4   The gold box 'floats' on top of the building
5   Powder room
6   Floor plan

8

8 Living room detail

9 Outdoor terrace with spectacular view of Melbourne at night

Photography: David B Simmonds

9

nou daquela vez
o se fosse a últim
da filho seu com
fosse o único
nçou e gargalho
o se ouvisse mús

EGREJA APARTMENT SÃO PAULO, BRAZIL ROSENBAUM — ARQUITETURA E INTERIORES

At 140 square meters, this is not a large apartment by São Paulo standards. Very cozy, with Brazilian contemporary flair, it is the result of close collaboration between the architect and the client, a collector of Brazilian art, who is also passionately moved by Brazilian popular music. Previously a city base for the client who lived on a farm, the apartment was transformed when she decided to make the city her home. A priority was to incorporate her extensive Brazilian art collection, which has been arranged like a patchwork around the apartment.

The walls of the apartment were opened to make one large space for the living, dining, and kitchen areas. A touch of whimsy is the poetry on the walls, part of a very famous song from well-known Brazilian composer and singer, Chico Buarque de Holanda. Snippets appear in the living space, in the entrance, and in the bedroom, poetry for a poetic soul.

The color palette is deliberately eclectic: the vibrant and colorful paintings of famous Brazilian artists contrast with the brown walls of the living space; the orange color of the curtain and the Egg chair enhances the black details in some items of furniture, which in turn anticipates the contemporary black kitchen.

1   Living room is wide and cozy and alive with color

2

3

2 Living room with blue wall adorned with
   song lyrics by Chico Buarque de Holanda

3 Dining table designed by the architects;
   18th-century Taiwanese horse separates
   dining area from living room

4 Large black pivot door opens to reveal
   wood latticework designed by the architect

5 Contemporary black kitchen

Photography: Douglas Garcia

4

ERIC STREET APARTMENT   COTTESLOE, WESTERN AUSTRALIA, AUSTRALIA   OVERMAN & ZUIDEVELD PTY LTD

The 250-square-meter apartment's layout creates an open-plan living area that relates to the adjoining 39-square-meter, north-facing balcony. Large areas of floor-to-ceiling glass between internal and external living areas make the internal areas feel larger. Bi-folding doors and large sliding doors allow internal and external areas to meld together into one large space.

A wide gallery space replaces the conventional passage linking the living areas to other rooms within the apartment. This space feels like a room in itself with doors set back from the wall face in recesses and the doors are located to provide maximum wall areas for artwork. A large pivot door allows the gallery to be separated from the entry if desired.

Through the use of raised ceiling areas and bulkheads, the large open-plan living area is zoned into living and dining/kitchen spaces. This manipulation of the ceiling also allows for variations in light source within each space.

The kitchen has a 'built-in' feel, rather than the look of cabinetwork added to the envelope. The cabinetwork is a dominant feature of the living space and provides a restrained non-utilitarian backdrop. There was a deliberate decision to avoid the use of wall tiles within the kitchen. Cabinetwork in the living room and entry was designed as an extension of the palette within the kitchen.

The materials selected for the interior of the apartment are generally from the gray color palette. Micro Cielo resin-based terrazzo was selected for the bench tops because of its durability and color. Queensland walnut was chosen as the timber veneer to add some warmth to the gray and neutral tones selected elsewhere. The dark carpet provides a strong visual base for the selected furniture. The ceilings of the balcony areas are lined with 'stressed' oak, which provides a weathered, driftwood feel, reflecting the beachside location.

Opposite

View from balcony to dining room with kitchen beyond

1 Adjoining apartment
2 Gallery
3 Lobby
4 Stairs
5 Lift
6 Entry
7 Living
8 Dining
9 Balcony
10 Kitchen
11 Bedroom 3
12 Bath
13 Bedroom 2
14 Walk-in-robe
15 Ensuite
16 Bedroom 1
17 Sitting
18 Sewing room
19 Laundry
20 Powder room

2

2 Floor plan
3 View of front and street entry
4 North-facing balcony with view to Indian Ocean

3

5

6

7

8

Photography: David Morcombe, Imagery Photographic Studio

9

10

11

FASHIONABLE LIVING   SÃO PAULO, BRAZIL   GILBERTO CIONI & OLEGÁRIO DE SÁ — ARQUITETURA E INTERIORES

The client spends part of the year in São Paulo, and part in Italy. His busy schedule required a very relaxed place to be when in São Paulo. The architects proposed a contemporary place with solid lines, sober, but very 2000s.

The 280-square-meter apartment has two floors with the living, dining and kitchen on the first floor, and the bedroom and television room on the second. A terrace covers almost the entire second floor, with 120 square meters of open space and a panoramic view of the city.

The walls in the first floor are white, with chamois in the dining space. A comfortable red couch breaks the monochromatic palette. The apartment is modern and functional. Everything works. The modern furniture for the first floor is a perfect match with the natural-fiber objects on the second. A wood floor covers the apartment and enters the kitchen where the ambience becomes 'chic'—fashion for the kitchen too.

The living area encourages conversation between friends with the red couch and an Egg chair. Behind the red couch a lounge space was formed with three ecological wood and leather chairs and a lacquered black coffee table. The black dining table forms a niche with its six wood and leather black chairs.

The special white gypsum roof covers all of the first floor and interacts with the original slab, forming geometric forms for the lighting. A white cement stair painted in white epoxy links both floors, and becomes another decorative feature, as is the black ebony door just below the staircase.

1   Dining room and home theater (gypsum detail)
2   Living room, dining room and lounge
3   Staircase detail
4   Upper view of stair

1

2

3

4

5

6

7

5   TV room on second floor
6   Living and dining room
7   Kitchen
8   Floor plan
9   View of São Paulo from TV room on second floor

Photography: Alexandre Kid

9

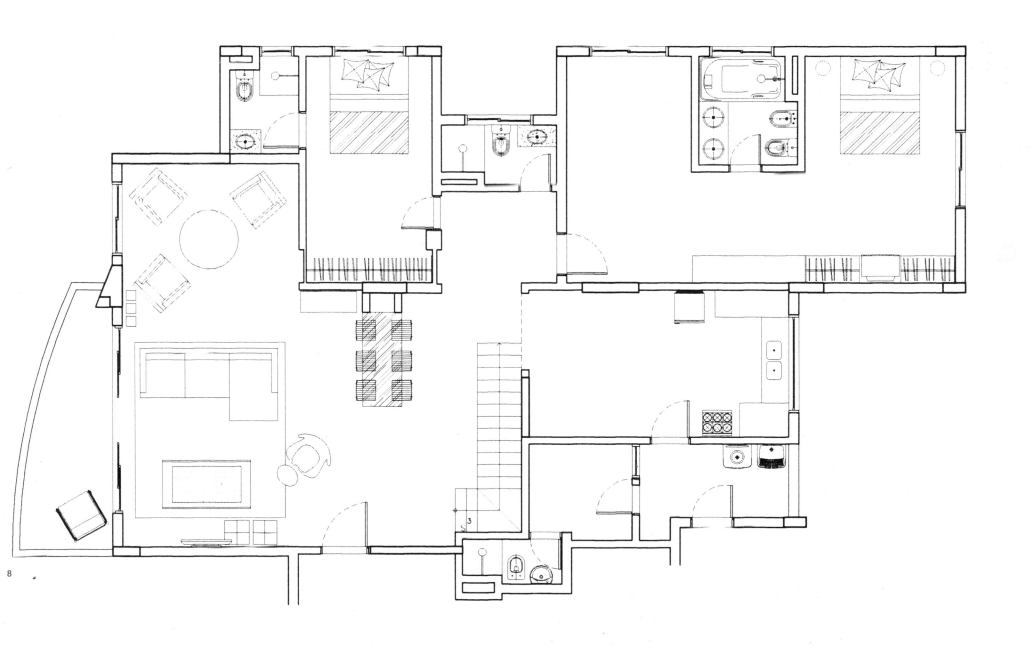

8

3

GLASS APARTMENT   SEATTLE, WASHINGTON, USA   OLSON SUNDBERG KUNDIG ALLEN ARCHITECTS

Glass, art, light, and water are recurring themes in this home for a collector of Northwest and Asian art. Using Puget Sound and the Pacific Ocean as a metaphorical setting to unite the collector's interests, the house takes on an organic and aqueous feeling. Located in a typical residential tower with relatively low ceiling heights, one of the design challenges was to create a sense of height and an open quality within a very tight envelope. Curved elements—made using floor-to-ceiling cast-glass walls, some of which incorporate glass display shelving for art—were introduced to reference shapes found in nature, and to draw the eye away from the physical limits of the space and onto the contents. Interior separations were kept to a minimum, or rendered in glass, to visually unify the interior.

Entering the foyer is like stepping out of a diving bell into an undersea world with bronze gates marking the threshold. Inside, light passing through the glass walls, as well as coming from within them, gives the interior spaces a luminous Northwest glow. Ceiling areas are lit to appear as if seen from below the surface of the water, further reinforcing the aquatic feeling of the space. Cabinetry and construction details are highly crafted reflecting the owner's dedication to the arts and crafts tradition the Northwest. Much of the furniture was custom-designed by Jim Olson and finds its inspiration in objects found while beachcombing: driftwood, lily pads (sawmill castoffs) and sea-polished glass. The architecture is intended to work in concert with the art—to hold the art but not be completely subordinated by it.

1   Curved window wall with luminous glass fins and shelves overlooking Puget Sound

2

3

4

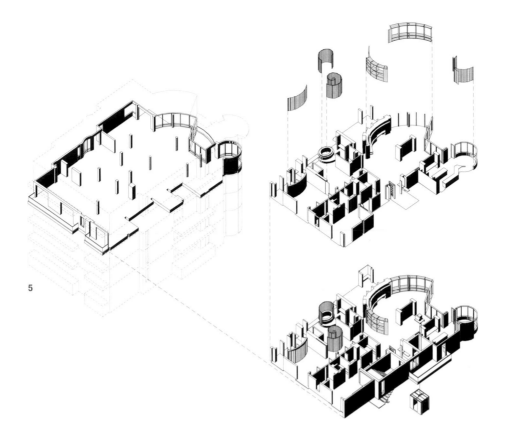

5

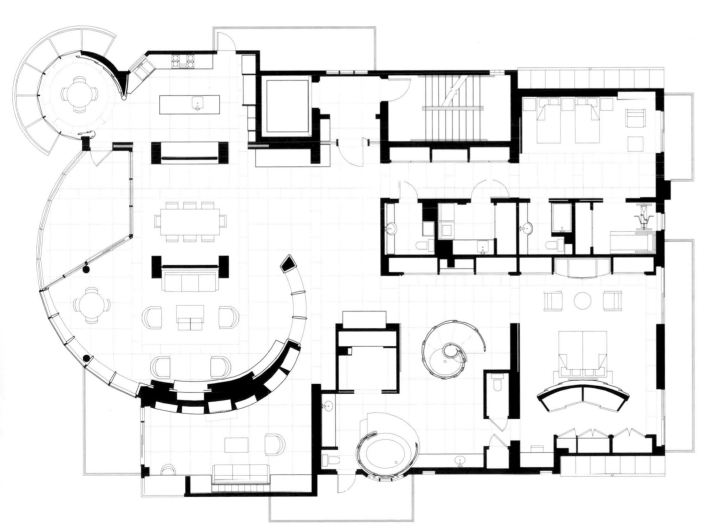

6

2 Entry foyer with bronze door
3 Hallway leading to guest suite
4 View from foyer toward den
5 Axonometric
6 Floor plan

7

8

9

10

11

12

13

Photography: Eduardo Calderon

16

15

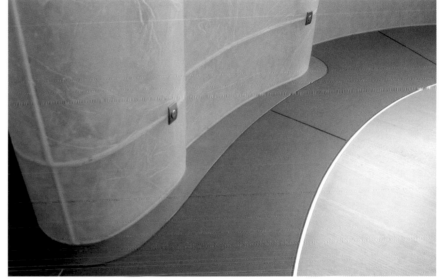

17

GREEN PENTHOUSE LOFT   NEW YORK, NEW YORK, USA   CHA & INNERHOFER ARCHITECTURE + DESIGN

The 1500-square-foot loft with a terrace is located on top of a 22-story residential high-rise. The terrace commands a view of the East Village, framed by the Queensboro Bridge to the north and the Manhattan Bridge to the south.

The clients, a young couple, who are both wine enthusiasts, requested a serene and open space to incorporate specific programmatic requirements ranging from daily living rituals to frequent entertaining.

The design strategy was to separate/articulate 'primary' and 'support' functions. The primary spaces are aligned and sequenced along the perimeter window wall, which acts as a porous plane with the living/kitchen/dining/master bedroom on the inside and the terrace on the outside. The visual perception of the perimeter window wall on the inside is a sequence of layered spaces, allowing the eye to traverse the length of the loft, through the apertures and transparencies of the furniture-like kitchen cabinetry as well as the glazed opening in the master bedroom wall.

The support spaces are arranged along the entry wall as closets, the powder room/master bathroom/walk-in closet, defining also the spatial perimeter of the primary spaces.

In between the primary and support spaces a continuous diagonal line of sight is preserved to emphasize the spatial depth of the interior, parallel to the expansive view from the terrace.

Light, materials, colors, and textures are used as a means of accentuating the visual and tactile experience of the loft, while references to the winemaking process provide abstracted forms and images. The use of materials such as the contrasting woods of ebony and ash of the kitchen cabinetry, in conjunction with the stone fountain providing a quiet stream of water, and the wood-clad circular wall of the powder room, enhances the sensual perception of the space and evokes a calming ambience.

Opposite
View of kitchen cabinetry opening to living room

3

2

2 Living room view from entry; white stained wood floor
   folds up to the wall and transforms into cove lighting
3 Living room view from terrace door
4 Kitchen, entry and powder room view from living room
5 Floor plan

4

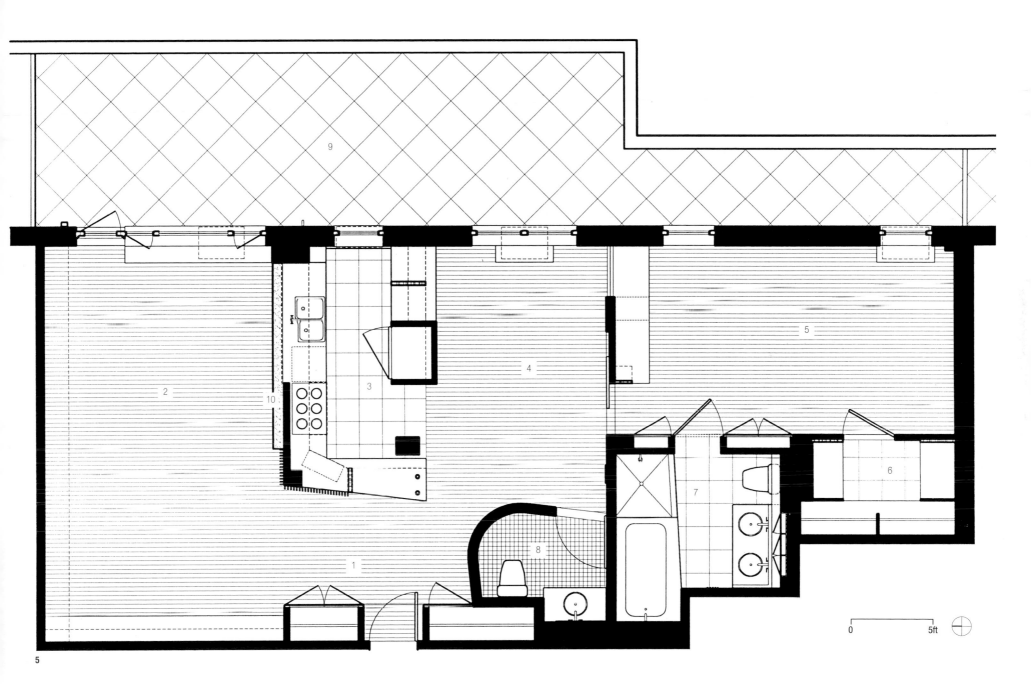

5

1   Entry
2   Living
3   Kitchen
4   Dining
5   Master bedroom
6   Walk-in closet
7   Master bathroom
8   Powder room
9   Terrace
10 Water trough

6

7

6   Dining room view; ash kitchen open cabinet counterbalances glazed opening at master bedroom wall

7   Kitchen view from living room, showing details of ebony upper cabinet and marble water trough

8   Master bedroom; folding maple work table engages kitchen's ebony upper cabinet through the sliding door

Photography: Dao Lou Zha

GREENWAY STREET APARTMENT PERTH, WESTERN AUSTRALIA, AUSTRALIA IREDALE PEDERSEN HOOK ARCHITECTS

This 100-square-meter project explores the role of time—past, present and future—and memory, short and long term.

Everyday acts of living are explored and celebrated—the light penetrating and brushing across a specifically placed chair, glass walls reflecting outside events, translucent plastic skins distorting events behind, glass floors permitting transparency between levels. Everything was considered and designed, including art, furniture, painting, cabinets, and lighting. Unexpected events occurred: light refracted into the color spectrum and then passed over paintings, unexpected reflections created new spatial qualities, and suddenly the spatial exploration was complete.

Evolving over a two-year period, the project was an opportunity to test, change and explore the use of color. Paint became an active participant in creating a dynamic world, a means by which time is registered, and layers of history reinterpreted, sometimes subtle (gloss white on white), sometimes bold.

The colour palette is composed of a primarily white background layered over existing cream painted walls with numerous painted 'events'. Materials used include Laminex anthracite for benchtops and cabinets; white colorbacked glass for splashbacks; Dulux Chinatown Orange lacquer finish for overhead cabinets; brushed stainless steel skirting; floors of local slate and special concrete, trowel-applied screed with three coats of water-based wax seal; pine tongue-and-groove flooring on upper levels.

1 Living space – electronic center and wall shadow

1

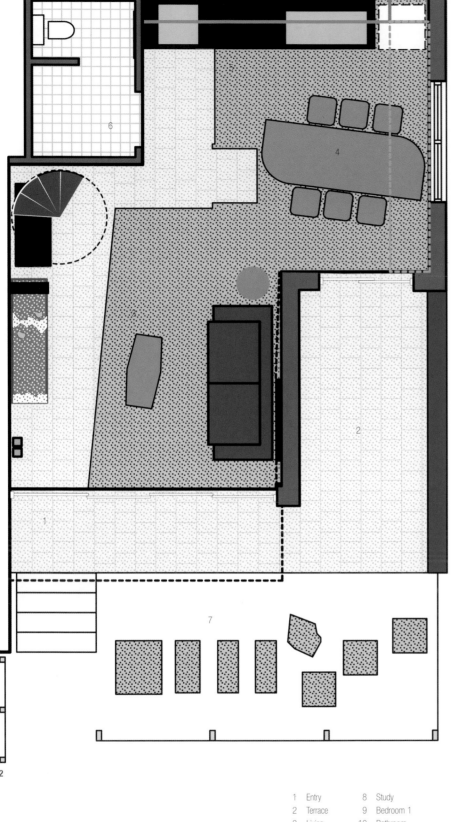

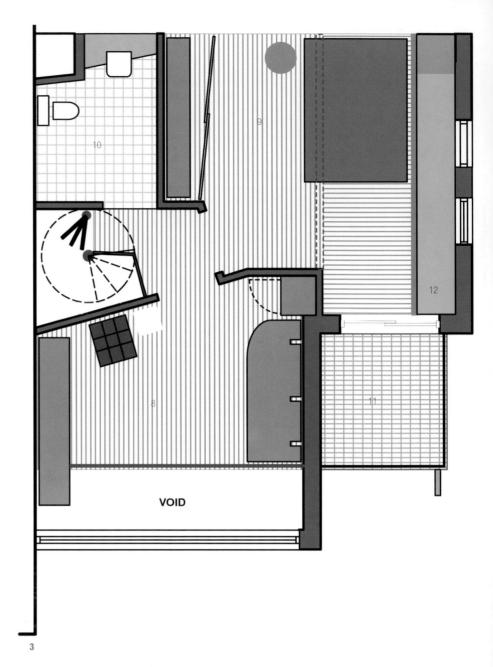

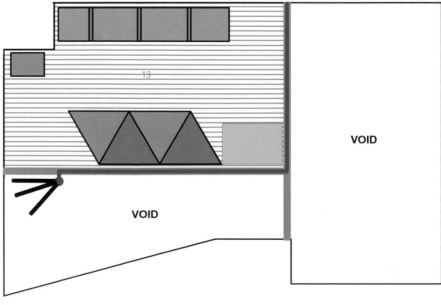

1	Entry	8	Study
2	Terrace	9	Bedroom 1
3	Living	10	Bathroom
4	Dining	11	Habitable sunscreen
5	Kitchen	12	Glass floor
6	Laundry	13	Studio/guest room
7	Garden		

VOID

VOID

VOID

5

6

7

2   Entrance level plan

3   Upper level plan

4   Mezzanine level plan

5   Bedroom glass floor

6   Study and specially designed artwork; recycled Australia Post signs with I-Mac monitor box and primitive art/figure

7   Register of sun's movement

8   Spiral ladder and stair

9   Kitchen cabinets and the ghost of past walls

Photography: Adrian Iredale

8

9

GYMNASIUM RESIDENCE   NEW YORK, NEW YORK, USA   GWATHMEY SIEGEL & ASSOCIATES ARCHITECTS

The 6000-square-foot apartment is located in the former gymnasium of the original Beaux Arts New York City Police Headquarters building.

The intention was to physically maintain and visually exploit the volumetric integrity and structural expression of the existing barrel-vaulted space, while adding a master bedroom suite and study/library balcony, and integrating an eclectic painting and sculpture collection.

On the main level of the 25-foot-high, steel trussed volume, is the multi-use living/dining/entertainment/gallery articulated by custom-designed, space-defining furniture. At the east end of the space is the master bedroom suite and study/library balcony accessed by an exposed stair, which rotates at the landing and runs parallel, behind the existing longitudinal steel truss, to attic guest bedrooms over the kitchen, master baths and dressing rooms.

The study/library balcony is suspended under the east end of the barrel vault and revealed from the master bedroom below, by a continuous radial skylight in the floor, expressing its separation while maintaining the volumetric extension.

The floor of the balcony defines the bedroom ceiling, floating asymmetrically within the existing orthogonal building frame, articulating its objectiveness and sectional variation.

Three large skylights were inserted into the south side of the barrel-vaulted roof, providing natural light into the longitudinal internal façade of the space and revealing the classic building pediment above.

Major materials used include Bateig limestone and oak plank floors, Venetian plaster walls, perforated glass fiber-reinforced gypsum, panels and plaster ceilings with white lacquer cabinets. The color palette comprises warm white walls, honey-stained wide plank oak floors, beige-gray limestone, brushed stainless steel, white lacquer cabinets, bluestone countertops, and walnut-stained cherry cabinets in the library.

1 View of living room from dining room

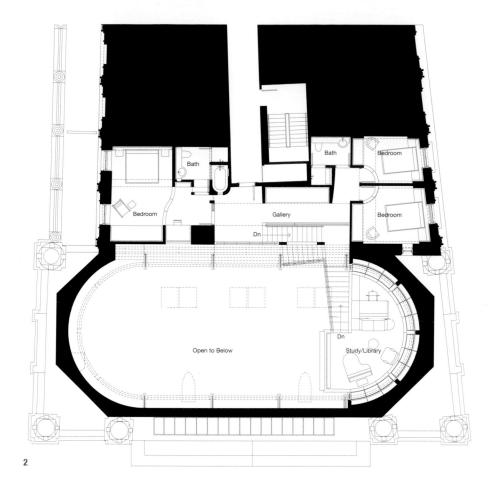

2

Bath

Bedroom

Bath

Bedroom

Bedroom

Gallery

Dn

Open to Below

Dn

Study/Library

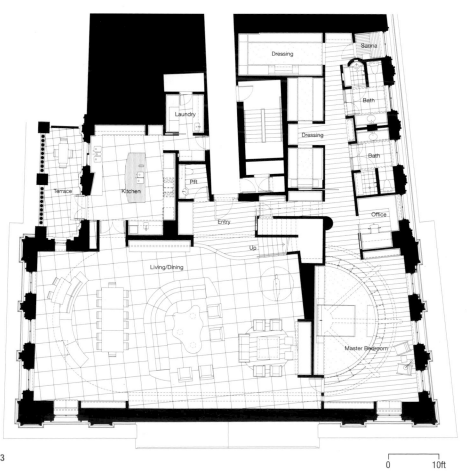

3

Dressing

Sauna

Laundry

Bath

Dressing

Bath

Terrace

Kitchen

PR

Office

Entry

Up

Living/Dining

Master Bedroom

0   10ft

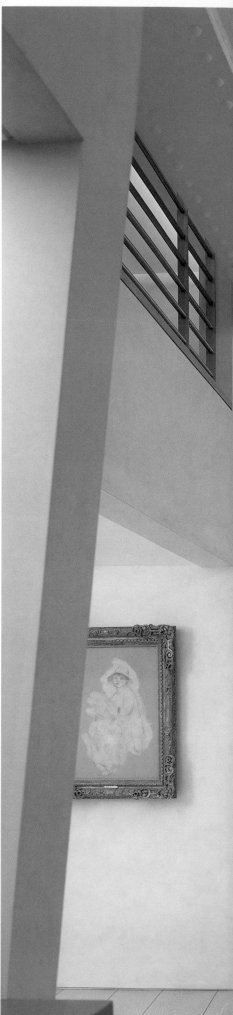

4

5

2 Second level plan
3 First level plan
4 Main entry
5 Existing conditions prior to renovation
6 Dining room

6

8

7

7   View of living room from breakfast area
8   Second-level balcony overlook with sculpture

9   Detail of library floor
10   Master bedroom, view toward headboard
Photography: Paul Warchol

HIGH STYLE IN SÃO PAULO   SÃO PAULO, BRAZIL   STUDIO HELENA VISCOMI

The owners of this 980-square-meter duplex apartment requested architect Helena Viscomi's help in remodeling their home by giving it 'a little flair and imagination.' Helena was struck by the living room's limitless possibilities. The huge space gave her the opportunity to relocate and organize all the objects of Oriental, Brazilian and European art that the couple has collected from their worldwide travels.

The clients have a very active social life so it was important to create a well-organized space. Warm in spirit, but slightly formal was the design brief. The two-story penthouse was designed some years ago, with two distinct levels: the first floor houses a covered terrace around the living room, the informal and formal dining rooms, five bedrooms, the kitchen and the service area and dog's area. Upstairs is the master bedroom with a private bathroom and private terrace, the home theater space, bar, swimming pool, barbecue, and the solarium from which one can admire a view of São Paulo city on the horizon.

The formal living room on the first floor is very classic and traditional, where the fine artworks are a perfect match for the silk sofas and curtains. The sweeping veranda can be used as an additional living room with chairs and sofas, or as a dining room, with its table for relaxed meals.

The home theater on the second floor, with its black and red color scheme contrasts to the traditional living room downstairs. Although it seems to be part of a completely different apartment, it fits perfectly with the needs of the different generations that live together.

1   Living room details: floor in Brazilian 'peroba rosa' wood, console with old blue and white Chinese porcelain and a Bidemeier table with a collection of family portraits

2

3

2 Terrace with night views of São Paulo city
3 Dining room, with 19th-century dining table and bronze chandelier
4 Home theater was designed for relaxing with family and friends
5 Home office and library
6 Bedroom for a university student
7 Living room detail

4

5

7

6

8

10

9

11

12

Photography: Martim William Szmick

HIGHLAND CONDOMINIUM SEATTLE, WASHINGTON, USA OLSON SUNDBERG KUNDIG ALLEN ARCHITECTS

Occupying the sixth floor of a mid-rise condominium on the south slope of Seattle's Queen Anne Hill, the Blem residence overlooks the downtown skyline and waterfront. The Space Needle commands the foreground, and Mount Rainier dominates the distance.

The owners, a couple with grown children, wanted refuge from the stress of their vocations. The husband manufactures medical imaging equipment, and this design embodies their love of clean lines and precision. It is restrained, using a monochromatic color palette and polished, elegant materials. Its planning is also simple and exact: a main room for living, cooking, eating, and entertaining, extends into subsidiary spaces such as bedrooms, a bathroom, and dressing and exercise areas. The absence of conventional walls and doors makes the moderately-sized space seem larger.

A curving, visually porous entry wall of perforated steel leads the eye into the apartment and creates a moiré pattern that changes as the viewer moves. Private space is separated from public by freestanding storage modules, sheathed in perforated metal, surmounted by uplights, and supported by steel brackets that extend from floor to ceiling. This row of volumes forms an axis that extends from the entry to the window wall at the opposite end of the apartment.

Primary finish materials include polished granite, glass block, and stainless steel, the latter forming the fireplace surround, much of the kitchen and bathroom, the bedroom headboard, and much of the flooring.

Details are highly crafted and articulated, and assume great prominence. The kitchen island, for example, is a sculptural plane of stainless steel tapering to a thin wafer at the end where it hangs from a suspended metal bar. In a city where interiors tend to be relaxed and organic, this apartment stands out with its finely honed Manhattan-like elegance.

1   Night view of dining and living rooms

2

3

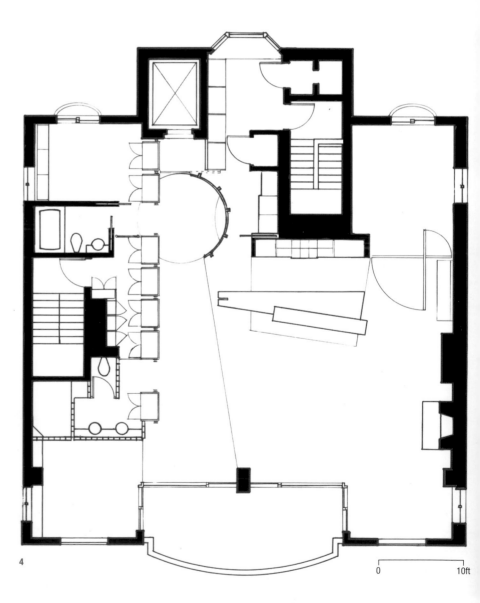

4

0　　　　　　10ft

2 Night view of dining and living rooms with cityscape beyond
3 View of kitchen and dining room
4 Floor plan
5 Kitchen with suspended buffet counter designed by Tom Kundig; all kitchen surfaces are stainless steel
6 Isometric

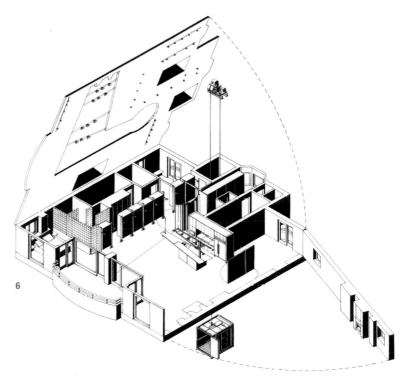

6

5

7

8

9

10

7 View toward kitchen
8 View from dining room to dressing cabinets. Glass block separates master bath from living space.
9 View from kitchen toward living room, highlighting stainless steel counter
10 Entry foyer

12

11 Master bathroom

12 Night view of bedroom; bed designed by Tom Kundig

Photography: Eduardo Calderón

HOOPER/MEYERSON RESIDENCE   NEW YORK, NEW YORK, USA   JANSON GOLDSTEIN LLP

Retention of the building's early 20th-century character was a priority for this apartment. An expansive loft space was not the goal, but a blend of openness and intimacy. A home that would allow the owners to express their love of fine arts, books and music. A color palette was developed from the Agnes Martin painting located at the entry. Fabrics, such as suede, cottons and linens were chosen for their texture and luxurious qualities.

At the center of the apartment is a glowing 'lantern' providing warm and ambient light. The lantern is made from fabric panels with incandescent lights recessed in the walls. The light source is hidden as well as the frame that supports the fabric. The lantern is best viewed in the living room from the suede-covered Barcelona chairs.

The master suite features a custom walnut bed designed by Janson Goldstein, and hanging fabric panels as window treatments. The panels, of cool blue/green create an ambient color in the room as natural light hits them. The bathroom features a limestone floor with a sandblasted slab for the shower, providing a sensation for the feet. The slab ends in a hidden trough where the water disappears.

1 View into living and dining area

1   Entry
2   Dining
3   Living room
4   Kitchen
5   Master bedroom
6   Master bathroom
7   Study
8   Bathroom
9   Guest room

3

2   View at living area with 'lantern'; Frank Stella print beyond

3   Floor plan

4

5

4   View from dining area; table custom-designed by Janson Goldstein and fabricated by Nicholas Mongiardo

5   Kitchen with dyed veneer cabinetry

6   View at dining area with Agnes Martin painting

7 Master bath with limestone floor
8 Master bedroom with walnut bed custom-designed by Janson Goldstein

Photography: Paul Warchol

7

JACKSON APARTMENT   SYDNEY, NEW SOUTH WALES, AUSTRALIA   STANIC HARDING ARCHITECTS

Prior to renovation this 150-square-meter apartment presented a low central corridor and a land-locked entry. Rooms ran along the perimeter of the building thereby denying the occupant connection to views, light and edge.

The apartment was opened by fusing circulation with habitable space. The planning allowed all major spaces to connect to the edge of the building and to views over Sydney Harbour. The incorporation of the external balcony and corridor space allowed for planning options that were not previously possible. The balcony now operates as a dining space but with the benefits of an outdoor space. It also links the main bedroom to the apartment in a way that reinforces its exclusion from the general living areas.

The design seeks to balance the connection to the extensive views and the focus on internal spaces. Joinery is used as a second layer to create elements that sometimes frame views and are sometimes the focus. These space-making elements are carefully detailed and connected; some are highly reflective and rich while others are plain and white. Color is used on walls and joinery furthest from the edge, with edge elements being white. Joinery wall paneling conceals services, storage, laundry and bathroom areas from the casual visitor. Discovering some of these items/areas enhances the space's experiential qualities. The use of mirrors also extends space and brings in the Harbour. The kitchen plays a central role as both space maker and viewing platform, reinforced by a change in floor level.

This project won the RAIA interior architecture award in 2003.

1   Complex form of kitchen is calmed by an all-white palette

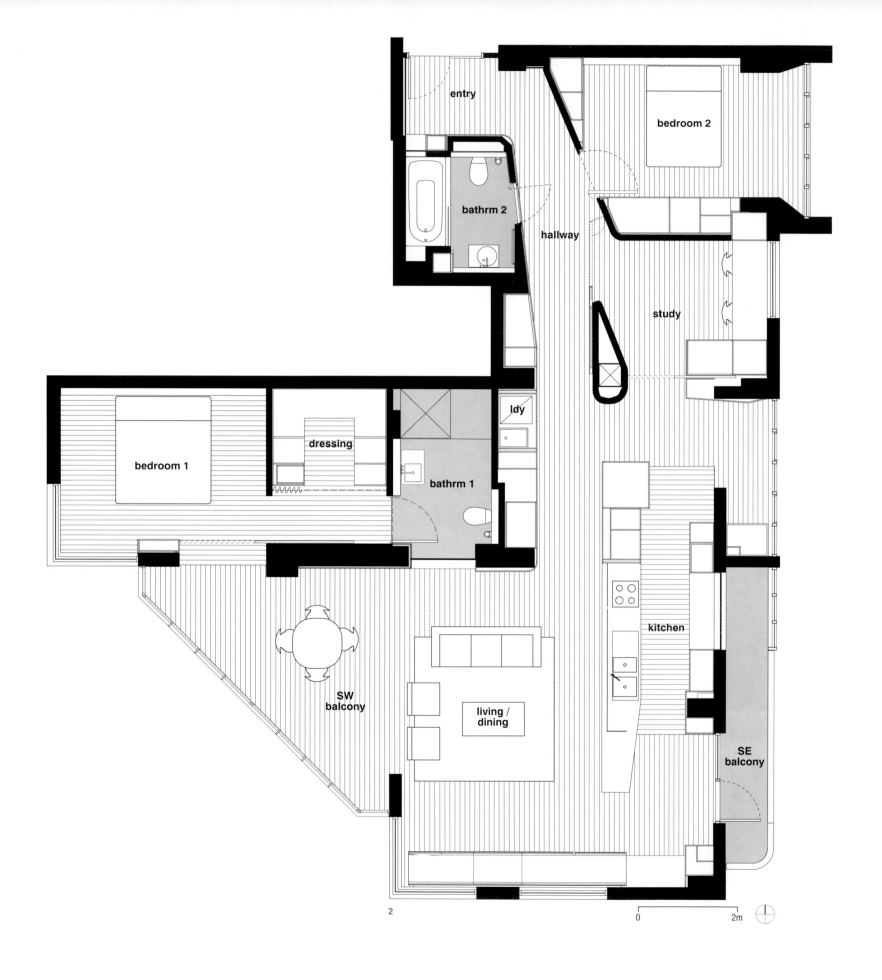

entry

bedroom 2

bathrm 2

hallway

study

bedroom 1

dressing

ldy

bathrm 1

kitchen

SW
balcony

living /
dining

SE
balcony

2

0   2m

3

4

2 Floor plan
3 Wenge base under floating credenza becomes corner cabinet
4 Floating silver credenza unit showing automated television lift in action

6

7

8

5 Harbour views are reflected and space is extended using mirrors

6 Standing at floating end of kitchen bench looking toward entry

7 Kitchen joinery extends along ceiling, note recessed aluminum finger slots

8 Entry to living space between white kitchen and wall paneling

9   Full-height translucent glass ensuite window illuminates dining space beyond
10 Colored glass and Corian-clad bathroom hidden behind corridor paneling
11 Passing full-height louvers of enclosed balcony to main bedroom
12 View to Walsh Bay from former balcony now dining space

Photography: Paul Gosney

9

10

11

12

LEHMAN PENTHOUSE LOFT   NEW YORK, NEW YORK, USA   CHA & INNERHOFER ARCHITECTURE + DESIGN

The 2000-square-foot loft occupies the top floor of a pre-war, 12-story manufacturing building in Chelsea, Manhattan.

The client, a record producer and banking executive, requested a live/work space that preserves and enhances the apartment's loft-like characteristics. The spatial and organizational hinge of the loft is the recording studio with a glass/steel enclosure that is perceived as a faceted lens reflecting the urban environment or as a luminous volume when lit from within. A curved glass/wood staircase wrapping around the studio leads up to the existing sunroom, on the roof level, which is defined by a glass/aluminum enclosure acting as a skylight. The volume of the studio divides the rectangular plan of the loft into two L-shaped halves: the public and the private. The public spaces—the entry/kitchen/dining, and living areas to the north are delineated by glass, open cabinetry and movable partitions. The private rooms—the study/ master bedroom/dressing room to the east, and the guest room/master bathroom/powder room to the south are enclosed by walls, storage cabinetry and opaque glass.

Both natural and artificial lighting are used in the design; during the day, natural light filters in through the east, west, north, and the skylight circulating further through colored glass transoms and apertures above doors. The natural light's refraction on, and coloration of, wood, glass, steel and stone reflects the outward views of the chaotic city environment. As the sun sets the process reverses, when the skin of the studio is illuminated by artificial lighting within the glass/steel framework, reorienting the spatial focus of the loft inward, to give the sense of a serene refuge from the hectic urban environment.

Opposite
View of glass mezzanine and glass stair from sunroom

2

2 Detail of glass stair treads with mahogany stair risers
3 Powder room with diffused lighting from glass stair above
4 View of glass studio/mezzanine wrapped by glass stair
5 Floor plan
6 View of glass stair, studio, entry and kitchen from dining room

3

4

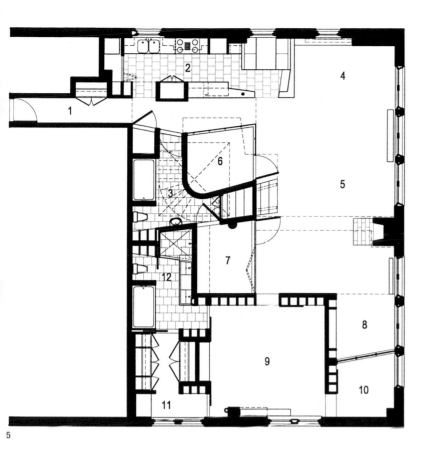

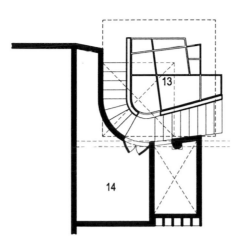

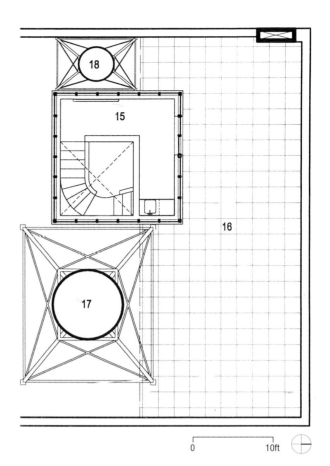

1 Entry	10 Study
2 Kitchen	11 Dressing room
3 Powder room	12 Master bath
4 Dining	13 Mezzanine
5 Living	14 Mechanical room/storage
6 Studio	15 Sun room
7 Guest room	16 Roof deck
8 TV room	17 Existing water tower
9 Master bedroom	18 Existing water tower

0   10ft

5

6

7

8

7 Entry is framed by kitchen and studio, with dining and living rooms beyond
8 View of kitchen's cherry/aluminum cabinetry with cast concrete countertop
9 View of studio with mezzanine above; kitchen and dining room beyond
10 Dining and living rooms, with studio, glass stair, guest room and master bedroom beyond
11 Living room is framed by glass studio

9

10

11

Opposite
   Master bath; rough cast concrete vanity, shower and floor constructions are punctuated by the delicate cherry cabinetry and mosaic tile insertions

13   Master bedroom with cherry sliding door/record shelves and built-in cherry headboard

Photographer: Dao Lou Zha

LIVING GALLERY   MELBOURNE, VICTORIA, AUSTRALIA   SJB INTERIORS

This 450-square-meter penthouse apartment is located on one of Melbourne's premier boulevards with access to abundant natural light and superb views of Port Phillip Bay, the Royal Botanic Gardens and the city skyline.

The project involved the refurbishment of an existing apartment with a conventional layout and standard finishes. The opportunity was provided to create a unique design, appropriate to the owners' specific lifestyle and an extensive collection of sculpture and art work that includes the bronze entry sculptures by artist Bronwyn Oliver.

The design concept adopts a clear expression of functions within the apartment. A raised stone platform in the entry sets up a defined circulation route through the center of the apartment and creates a dramatic transition into the spacious living areas. Services, storage and structural elements are combined in simple, geometric forms to create sculptural objects within the space. Storage units are built into passage walls, and large mirror panels are strategically positioned to enhance and extend the illusion of space and views.

The material palette and finishes consist of honed natural limestone, dark timbers (solid and veneers) and the luster of chrome and transparent glass, which create a sense of calm and comfort. Furniture was chosen for its simplicity, classic modernist design and grouped to define separate living zones. The entire apartment evokes the feel of a living gallery while still reinforcing the strong presence of the outside views.

1   Informal living area incorporating customized joinery unit to separate kitchen and meals area beyond

2   View from formal living area overlooking dining area

3   Full-height pivot door provides privacy to master bedroom

1

2

3

4

5

6

4   View along corridor with concealed storage cupboards and access
    to master bedroom suite
5   Detail view of living areas
6   Entry platform framed by columns and lowered ceiling
7   Floor plan

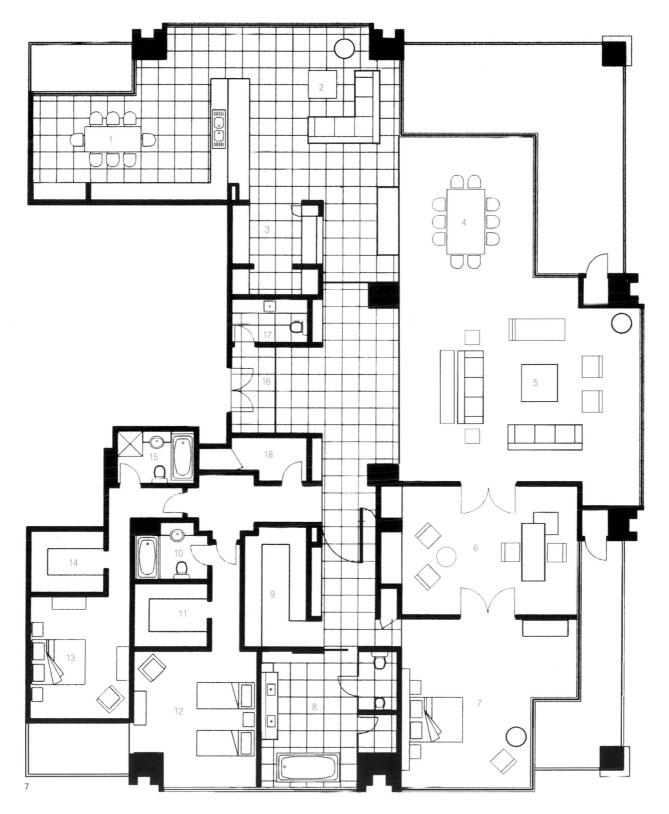

1   Informal dining/kitchen
2   Informal living
3   Bar
4   Formal dining
5   Formal living
6   Study
7   Main bedroom
8   Main ensuite
9   Wardrobe
10   Bathroom
11   Wardrobe
12   Bedroom
13   Bedroom
14   Wardrobe
15   Bathroom
16   Main entrance
17   Powder room
18   Laundry

8

9

8 Full-height mirrors, translucent glass and cantilevered vanity create a luxurious feel in the ensuite bathroom

9 Custom-made stone spa bath overlooks extensive view

10 View of apartment entry with dramatic suspended bronze sculptures

11 Detail of formal living area

12 Subdued atmosphere created by library and leather seating in study

Photography: James Grant

11

10

12

LIVING IN THE CITY   MELBOURNE, VICTORIA, AUSTRALIA   FENDER KATSALIDIS PTY LTD

The view is a tall city structure with a backdrop of Melbourne's leafy Eastern suburban grain meeting the rolling wall of the Dandenong Ranges. Dusk is luminous orange reflections of sunset on the towers with evening firing up the kinetic red tail-lights of cars retreating to suburbia. The sky is ever changing; fog which turns windows into surreal white opaque screens; racing cumulus formations; hot air balloons and orange suns.

Every day is vivid and inspiring.

This is the joy of high-rise apartment living. This apartment seeks to highlight the external visual palette and absorb the structure of the city in a sculpturally contrapuntal representation. The internal architecture encourages changing light and shadow patterns, to live and breathe its privileged location. Black and white prevail, contrasting the kaleidoscope colors outside.

Walls and ceilings reject the notion of simple sub-divisional presence, becoming sculptural elements, muscling space and manipulating ebb and flow of the internal volume and circulation. External panoramas form the art of the house. The two-story volume of the living area heightens the experience of sky meeting city, and to enhance the internal/external visual connectivity.

Ceilings, which distribute services, have been treated as cubist forms, interlocking, overlapping and becoming walls to create view frames and the element of surprise.

The lower level, which comprises kitchen, dining, living and study, is planned for visual connectivity during the various activities of family members. The upper level contains three bedrooms, associated bathrooms and a media mezzanine that overlooks the living area below.

The apartment has a balcony to its total perimeter, which expands into a double-height volume adjacent to the living and stud; this again magnifies the relationship of the apartment and the occupants within the city.

1   Living area has panoramic views over Melbourne

2

3

4

5

2 Lower level floor plan
3 Upper level floor plan
4 Living area
5 Platform to stair
6 Living area at dusk
7 Kitchen island, seen from dining area

6

7

8

8   Dining area
9   Top-floor swimming pool has views to Melbourne's east and west
10 Swimming pool

9

10

11

11   Kitchen island bench detail

12   Kitchen island bench

Opposite
   Night view from terrace

Photography: David B Simmonds

12

LOFT 6 SYDNEY, NEW SOUTH WALES, AUSTRALIA   DALE JONES-EVANS PTY LTD ARCHITECTURE

Loft 6 is one of ten lofts forming part of the 50–54 Ann Street Warehouse Loft Conversion, also designed by the architect. The shell space was completely replanned and detailed by the architect; the design creates a seductive gallery for functional living and pays great attention to drama and light.

The approach was to re-structure the ground plane as a cavernous sinew of spaces and make the floor solid, so one felt grounded—earthed. The three-story void and main place of ascension was then reinforced through cantilevering and floating the main stairs and using slatted timbers for landings and bridges.

The interior utilizes a painterly palette of surfaces to offset the owners' art collection. The layout of bedrooms below and living spaces above generated the off-white to black-brown color scheme. The spaces below are cave-like and white, while the higher-level floors remain in timber and stained off-black, contrasting with the solid white cavern below. This dark ceiling and floor in the living spaces tempers the intensity of the east–west light, visually extending the space toward the external deck and water-garden. The water-garden is replenished through a talon of copper as part of a cooling and decorative device for the living spaces.

In the sunroom above, light is filtered through a bamboo screen to reinforce the presence of light and sky. The roof level acts as a place to connect with non-urban elements in full view of the city and is also a place for contemplation.

2

2 Living to kitchen and suspended stair
3 Roof deck and bamboo-screened sun room
4 Dining/living area floor plan
5 Roof plan
6 Entry level floor plan

3

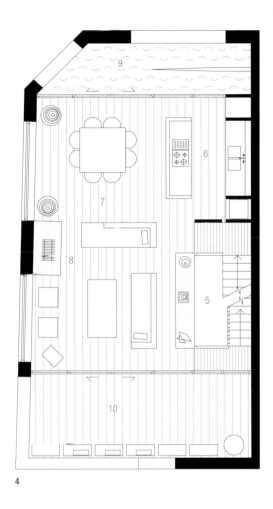

4

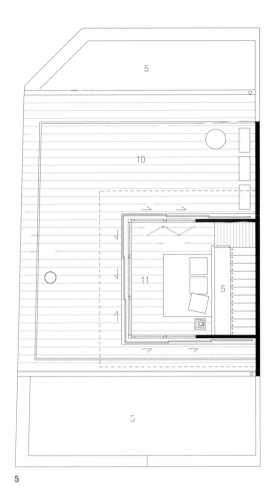

5

6

1   Gallery (entry)
2   Bedroom
3   Bathroom
4   Laundry
5   Void
6   Kitchen
7   Living/dining
8   Fireplace
9   Water feature
10 Deck
11 Sun room

7

7 Main bedroom with curved wall and gallery/robe
8 Kitchen
9 Entry void/stair gallery
10 Black pebbled pool with copper talon
11 Caved entry with Indian light Jalis
12 Living room

Photography: Giorgio Possenti (1,3,8,9,12); Willem Rethmeier (10); Jeremy Simons (2,7,11)

8

9

10

12

11

LOS ANGELES RESIDENCE   LOS ANGELES, CALIFORNIA, USA   MITCHELL FREEDLAND DESIGN

'Contemporary' and 'chic' were the marketing directions for this luxury condominium model suite located in a prominent new high-rise tower.

The design intent of the two-bedroom, 2700-square-foot unit was for it to have strong visual impact. This was achieved through the use of high contrast red, bone and black elements, which give the principal rooms a kinetic crackle. Furniture throughout the suite is custom-designed and inspired by French design icons from the 1920s and 1940s. The use of strong contemporary art juxtaposed with Asian artifacts produces the illusion that the space is inhabited by an individual with definite tastes.

The original entry foyer was bland and devoid of architectural interest. A separation was implemented between the foyer and living room to establish order and a sense of arrival. This provides a defined transition between finishes and space. The ceiling was dropped and lighting added to heighten the drama upon arrival. Pale colored French limestone flooring was used throughout the principal rooms to unify the space and visually expand the floor plan. Recessed lighting was introduced into the existing ceiling plan to accent the art and furniture collections.

The master bathroom was intentionally designed to provide contrast to the rest of the suite, employing a soft white-on-white palette. This room provides an ethereal end to the passage through a strong, visually stimulating environment. The journey ends on a subliminally seductive note, fulfilling the marketing objective of dynamic modernity and serene chic.

1   Front entry hall

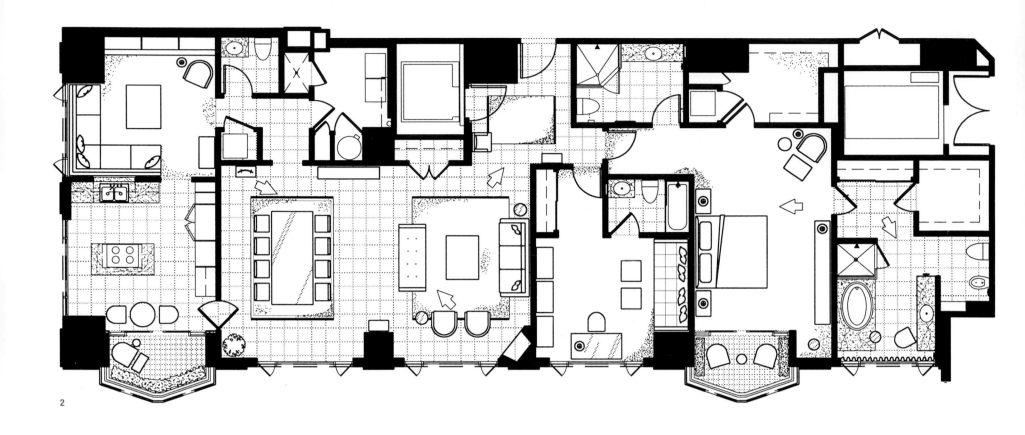

2

3

4

5

6

7

7   Living room
8   Dining area
9   Master bedroom

Photography: Ed White Photographics

8

MODERN STYLE   SÃO PAULO, BRAZIL   GUI MATTOS ARQUITETURA

Gui Mattos' client was accustomed to living in and planning big, open houses so it was a challenge to plan the smaller space of an apartment. Fortunately, the close affinity between architect and client made the transition a positive experience.

The owner, an enthusiastic collector of modern art and design, wanted something to fit his contemporary lifestyle. The first thing to do was to make the apartment as cozy and home-like as his previous residence.

The architect opened the walls to make one large space for the living and dining areas. Fabulous objects d'art and artworks make this a balanced, unified space. A feature of the apartment was the abundance of natural light, which contributes to the overall ambience, especially in the living areas, with their floor-to-ceiling windows.

Some significant changes to the original plan were made to adapt the space to the owner's style of living. Some interior finishes were changed, to enhance the display of the paintings and other works of art.

Opposite
Living room, with central table designed by the architect

3

4

5

6

2 General view of living room with dining room beyond
3 Living room artworks: white painting by Jane Harries and pair of black leather chairs by Dotto
4 Spectacular pivot glass door in the entrance
5 Living room furnishing detail
6 Dining room lamp detail

7

8

9

10

11

7   Living room features black low buffet and Ianelli painting
8   Dining room
9   Red cushions contrast with the double white sofas
10 Dotto chair; painting by Milton Dacosta in background
11 Living room, with central table designed by the architect

Photography: Tuca Reines

OLIVER LANE PENTHOUSE   MELBOURNE, VICTORIA, AUSTRALIA   DESIGNINC MELBOURNE

The brief for this project called for a reinvention of the interior. Previously renovated in the mid 1990s, the existing interior had become tired and dated. The client requested a timeless design that would not date so readily. A refurbishment of an existing penthouse in the Melbourne CBD, this project included upgrading the existing kitchen and designing a new bathroom. Through structural alteration and furniture specification, this project succeeded in meeting the client's requirements and creating a light, bright, inviting environment. Combining new furniture items with reupholstered existing pieces, the design demonstrates a successful synergy between new and old. Existing carpet and kitchen tiles were removed to achieve a seamless spotted gum timber floor throughout the apartment, creating a sense of expansion.

Classic modern furniture pieces were selected and the upholstery palette focused more on texture and depth than color, giving the apartment an added dimension in tactility. New lighting systems were also specified to further enhance the open plan, together with the replacement of internal walls with frameless glass panels to maximize natural light and promote visual connections between rooms and city skylines.

A highlight of the apartment is the ensuite bathroom that features frameless glass panels, stainless steel mosaic tiles and a ceramic 'box' vanity. The minimal palette used in the refurbishment artistically blends all elements of the apartment, old and new, into a contemporary reinvention of the penthouse.

1 Casual living—glazed screens to bedrooms

2

2 Panoramic view of casual living, kitchen and dining areas with formal lounge beyond
3 View to formal lounge
4 Floor plan

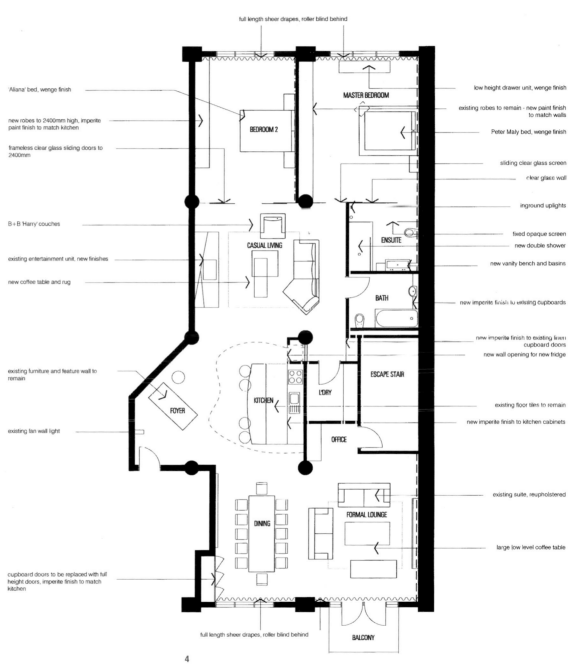

full length sheer drapes, roller blind behind

'Aliana' bed, wenge finish

low height drawer unit, wenge finish

MASTER BEDROOM

new robes to 2400mm high, imperite paint finish to match kitchen

existing robes to remain - new paint finish to match walls

BEDROOM 2

Peter Maly bed, wenge finish

frameless clear glass sliding doors to 2400mm

sliding clear glass screen

clear glass wall

inground uplights

B+B 'Harry' couches

CASUAL LIVING

ENSUITE

fixed opaque screen

new double shower

existing entertainment unit, new finishes

new vanity bench and basins

new coffee table and rug

BATH

new imperite finish to existing cupboards

new imperite finish to existing linen cupboard doors

new wall opening for new fridge

existing furniture and feature wall to remain

ESCAPE STAIR

FOYER

KITCHEN

L'DRY

existing floor tiles to remain

existing fan wall light

new imperite finish to kitchen cabinets

OFFICE

existing suite, reupholstered

DINING

FORMAL LOUNGE

large low level coffee table

cupboard doors to be replaced with full height doors, imperite finish to match kitchen

full length sheer drapes, roller blind behind

BALCONY

4

3

5

6

5 Master bedroom with view to ensuite
6 Dining
7 Second bedroom
8 Ensuite

Photography: David B Simmonds

8

7

PERRATON APARTMENT   SYDNEY, NEW SOUTH WALES, AUSTRALIA   STEPHEN VARADY ARCHITECTURE

The design for this city apartment set out to explore an intensive, practical use of space through sculptural and formal exploration, to not only make a 40-square-meter apartment more practical and functional, but also make it appear larger.

The design approach treats the interior as a series of intersecting, white rectangular prisms—initially suggested by the strong rectilinear form of the existing envelope. The intent was to hide what was not necessary, only bringing it to life when needed. For example, the kitchen does not look like a kitchen, but a sculptural wall of intersecting elements, stepping back and forth to accommodate storage, appliances and plumbing, with certain parts folding down, sliding out or opening to reveal the various functions related to the preparation of food.

The design also explores other ideas for saving space. Select sections of the non-load-bearing walls, as well as the bedroom and bathroom doors have been removed and replaced with large sliding panels. The cantilevered dining table folds away to become part of the overall composition, allowing clear floor space when it is not in use. The television has been encased in a sculptural cabinet and suspended from a box on the ceiling which completely conceals the power and antenna cables, and a sliding track allows it to glide along the ceiling.

A number of strategically placed mirrors also allow the apartment to appear more than what it is. The major mirror beside the main northern window not only extends the perception of space, but it brings a previously limited view of Sydney Harbour right inside the apartment.

The kinetic potential of spaces intersecting is consciously explored; thus, the design is never fixed, never static, allowing the apartment to vary in size, proportion and mood depending on the required or desired function.

1   Living area with reflected view of Sydney Harbour
2   Sliding sculptural television unit – closed
3   Sliding sculptural television unit – open
4   View of living and dining area toward kitchen with dining table folded away
5   View of dining and living area

1

4

2

3

5

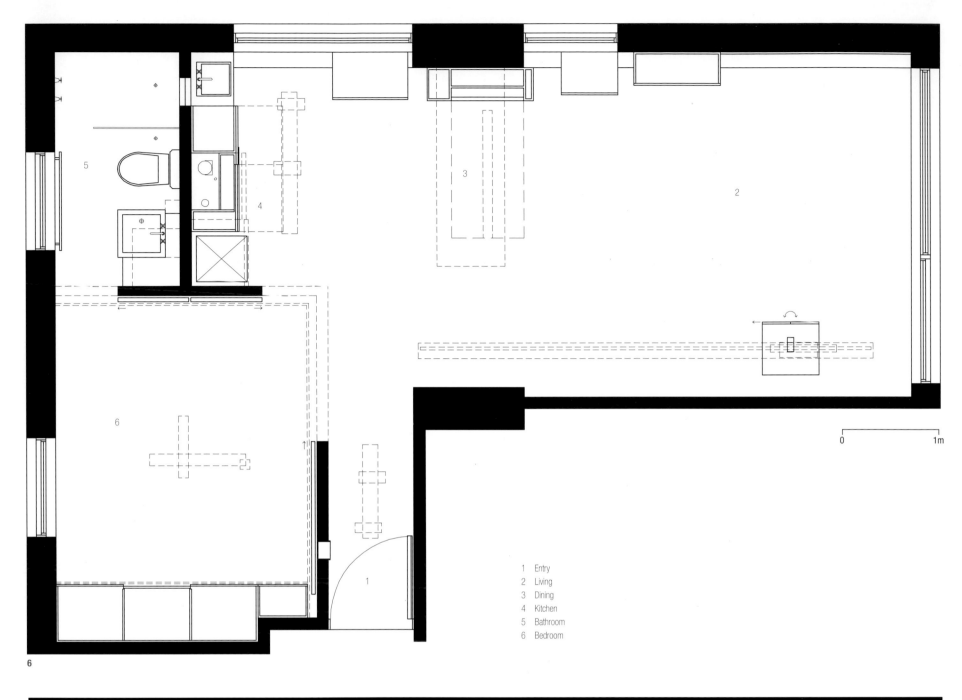

1 Entry
2 Living
3 Dining
4 Kitchen
5 Bathroom
6 Bedroom

6

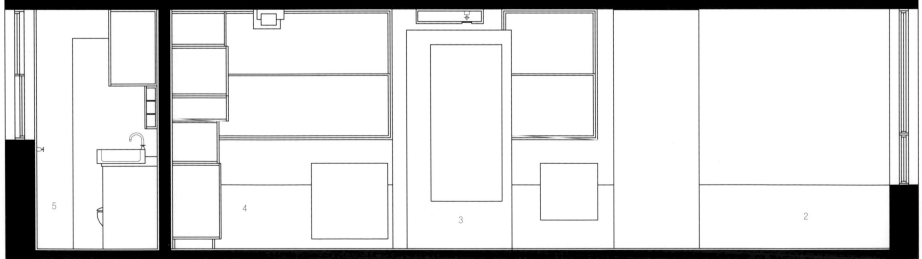

7

8

9

10

6 Floor plan
7 Section
8 View to bedroom – sliding doors closed
9 View to bedroom – one sliding door open
10 View to bedroom – both sliding doors open
11 Kitchen detail – closed
12 Bathroom detail
13 'Arkhitekton' light detail

Photography: Stephen Varady

11

12

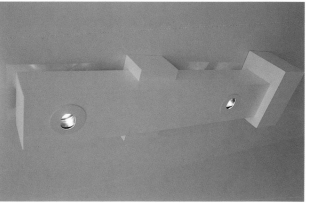

13

POD MELBOURNE, VICTORIA, AUSTRALIA STEPHEN JOLSON ARCHITECT PTY LTD

This 250-square-meter project challenges the traditional notions of home, space, and living.

Perceived as a seemingly autonomous entity, the 'pod' floats between the existing floor and ceiling, cushioned by dark shadows, and articulated by plays of natural light. Each junction has been carefully articulated to maintain the purity of simple forms. Each zone is pressed into the solid container.

Floors become stages; rooms without walls.

The deliberate placement of the 'pod' divides the warehouse into two realms: a public façade with crisp, lineal features, and a private retreat where the intimate spaces play with tactile textures. The experience is an interplay of open space, juxtaposing forms, lightness and darkness.

A basic color scheme of contrasting shades of white and dark, shadow and light is reflected in the predominant materials: plasterboard, stained timber flooring, Tretford carpet and Statuaria marble.

1   Lounge area with modular couch and open natural fireplace

1 Entry
2 Living
3 Dining
4 Master bedroom
5 Dressing
6 Bathroom
7 Laundry
8 Powder
9 Study/bedroom 2

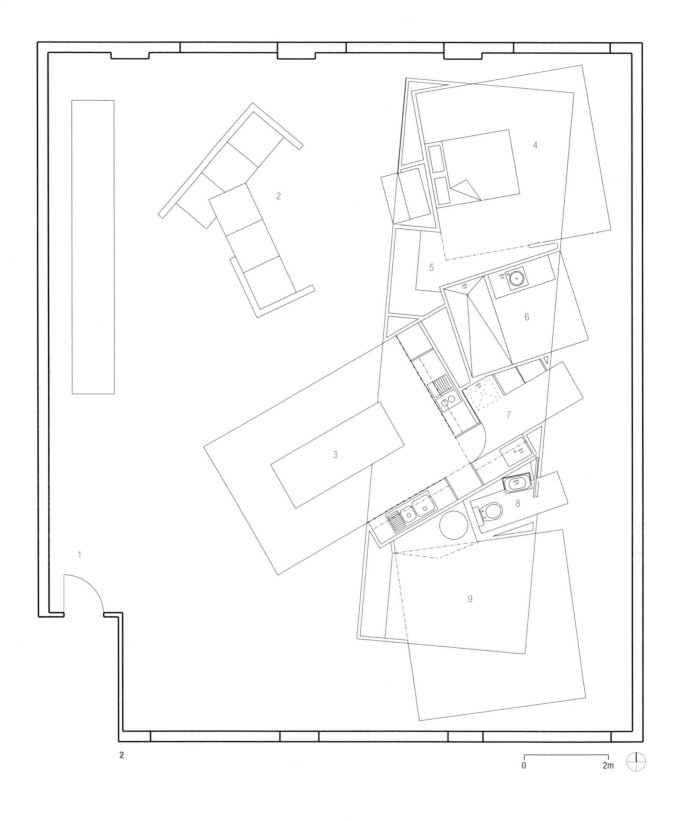

2

0   2m

3

4

2 Floor plan

3 Public realm of the Pod; kitchen, dining and lounge area

4 Passage to private realm of the Pod

5

5 Master bedroom with 'veiled' walls which conceal walk-in robe
6 Floating shelf and artwork by architect
7 Private realm of the Pod; bedrooms, laundry and bathrooms
8 Shadow and light detail
9 Main bathroom with translucent screen
Photography: Tim Griffith

6

7

8

9

POTTER'S PAD   NEW YORK, NEW YORK, USA   RESOLUTION: 4 ARCHITECTURE

Located in New York's Chelsea neighborhood, this 1400-square-foot loft renovation responds to the client's reductive lifestyle. The main volume is sheathed by a series of planes intended to articulate the edges and thresholds of the space. Within this volume, zones of use are suggested by the placement of specific planes of material. A raised plane of concrete ceiling panels identifies the living zone. Flanked by an anchored wall of steel and a floating wall of plaster, the dining zone is registered by a penetrating wedge of light from above, while a slipped plane of stone defines the fireplace to one side. Kitchen cabinets and appliances occupy a bite out of the central core and form another edge to the main open volume. Kitchen and dining zones are unified by a series of dancing rectangular bars of light that are carved into the ceiling above.

Thresholds of the space are layered with planes that slide, pivot, and roll. The sliding 'front door' provides security as a custom steel panel notched for hardware and light switches. The pivoting bedroom door provides privacy from within, while allowing light and a continuous brick wall to slip past, connecting the full length of the loft. Rolling perforated window scrims diffuse sunlight and provide privacy from the outside, while maintaining a view of the street.

Additional 'planes of use' fold, cantilever, and divide. An additional sleeping plane for guests folds into a concealed cabinet in the living zone. The master bed is composed of several cantilevered planes, and storage cabinets are accented with aluminum dividers. Sliced with aluminum, a slab of Baltic ply is used as a dining table that is equipped with industrial casters. It has the ability to roll up against the kitchen island and clear the space for impromptu dancing.

1 View of dining toward kitchen

1

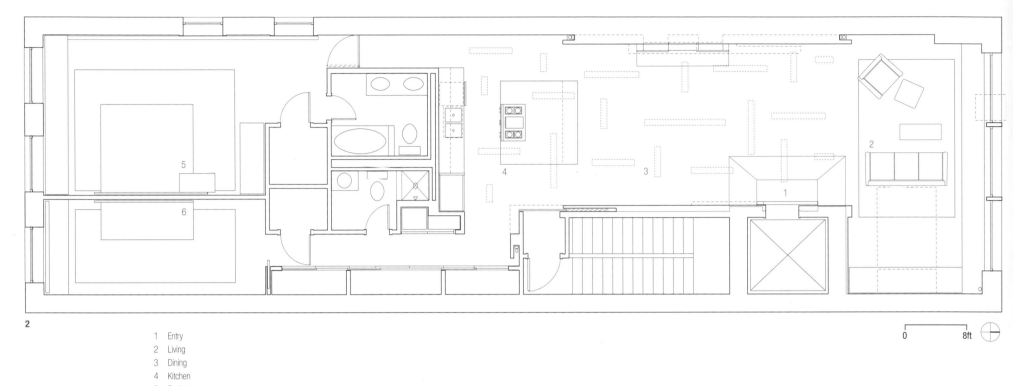

2

1   Entry
2   Living
3   Dining
4   Kitchen
5   Bedroom
6   Guest bedroom

0   8ft

3

2   Floor plan
3   Black steel fireplace detail
4   Bedroom lumasite doors
5   View from kitchen toward living
6   Steel entry door

4

5

6

9

10

8

11

Photography: courtesy Resolution: 4 Architecture

13

14

ROOMS WITH A VIEW – MELBOURNE PENTHOUSE   MELBOURNE, VICTORIA, AUSTRALIA   SJB INTERIORS

Located in a recently completed residential tower, this 1200-square-meter, two-level penthouse enjoys extensive views over Port Phillip Bay, adjacent parklands and many of Melbourne's major landmarks.

The design of this luxury apartment, extending over the upper levels of the building, optimizes the owner's opportunity to appreciate the various distant views from all parts of the floor. Rooms and circulation zones are arranged to allow dramatic and extended internal vistas through the apartment to the outside world. The elegant and sophisticated design recently won the major award from the 2004 Interior Design Awards Australia.

Large sliding panels and pivot doors retract and/or revolve to open up private living areas into large, entertaining spaces including an art gallery and home theater. The focus of the entry hall is a concrete spiral stair leading to a self-contained guest wing and bedroom on the upper level. This limestone-clad stair, finished with a waxed Venetian stucco and stainless steel mesh handrail, provides a visual centerpiece for both occupants and visitors arriving or moving through the apartment. Long, continuous walls clad in various materials (including bronze-finished brass, upholstered fabric panels and gloss white paintwork) conceal the entry points to powder rooms and bedrooms while also providing the dramatic backdrop for an extensive art collection.

The living areas, including two lounges, a dining room, bar and library occupy one end of the lower level, including a double-height volume with a study above. Accessed by a dramatic timber stair, this upper-level study opens onto a rooftop terrace including extensive seating areas and a glass swimming pool.

The palette of materials and colors was selected to create a vibrant yet restful character for the apartment interior. Dark stained timber platforms and limestone flooring combine with individually designed, patterned carpet to form the base for selected furniture, lighting and feature walls.

A focus on craftsmanship and detailing throughout the apartment, together with dramatic internal volumes and external views, combine to ensure a memorable experience somewhere 'between heaven and earth.'

1   Roof-top terrace with raised timber platform and glass-sided swimming pool
2   Gallery exhibition space

1

2

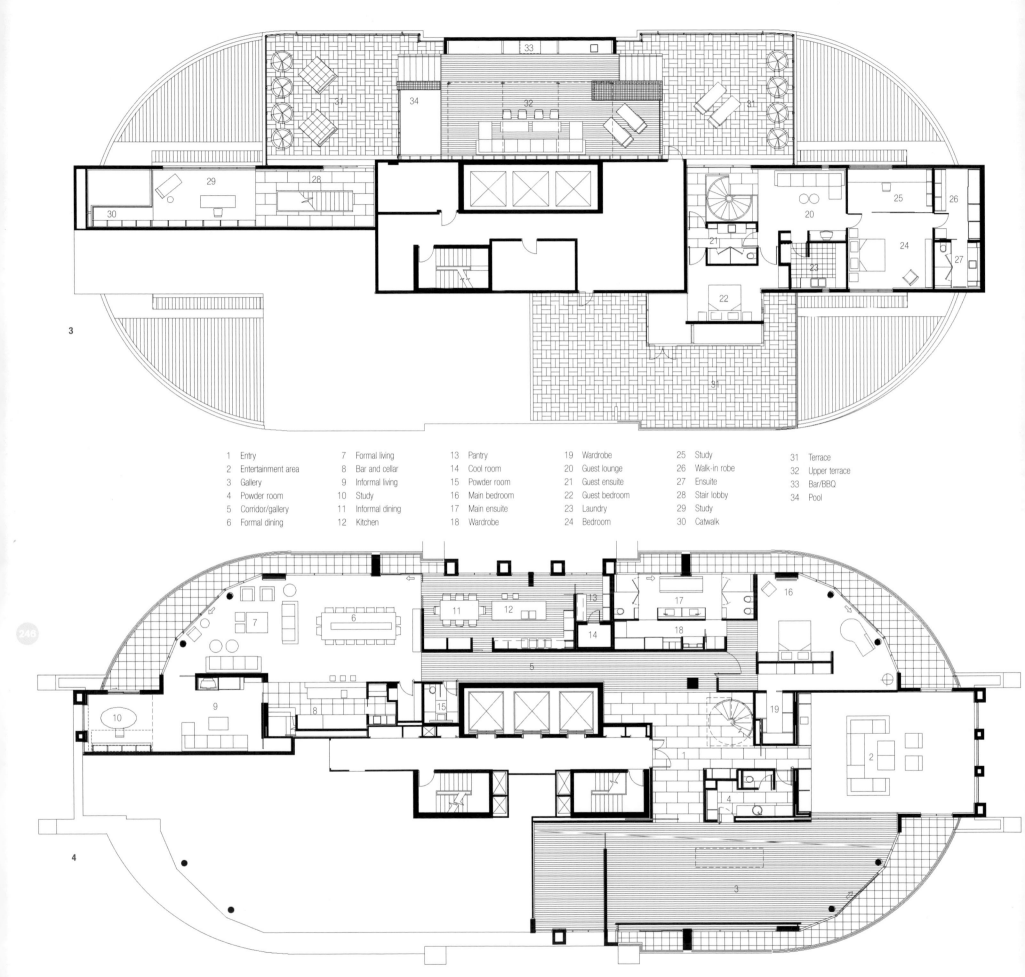

1	Entry	7	Formal living	13	Pantry	19	Wardrobe
2	Entertainment area	8	Bar and cellar	14	Cool room	20	Guest lounge
3	Gallery	9	Informal living	15	Powder room	21	Guest ensuite
4	Powder room	10	Study	16	Main bedroom	22	Guest bedroom
5	Corridor/gallery	11	Informal dining	17	Main ensuite	23	Laundry
6	Formal dining	12	Kitchen	18	Wardrobe	24	Bedroom

25	Study	31	Terrace
26	Walk-in robe	32	Upper terrace
27	Ensuite	33	Bar/BBQ
28	Stair lobby	34	Pool
29	Study		
30	Catwalk		

3

4

246

5

3 Upper floor plan
4 Lower floor plan
5 Entertainment room and gallery beyond
6 Guest powder room with silk upholstered walls and stainless steel mesh screen.
   Custom-made stone basin inserted in full-height mirror panel.

6

7 Apartment entry featuring concrete spiral stair
8 Rear timber stair with recessed wall lighting
9 Spiral stair viewed from upper level

8

9

10

11

12

13

14

10 Formal dining area with bar and living room beyond
11 Formal living area
12 Detail of bar with built-in fish tank
13 Custom-made stone bath in main ensuite
14 Powder room with silk upholstered walls, cantilevered limestone vanity and stone 'Boffi' basin
15 Master bedroom with silk upholstered bedhead
16 Main ensuite bathroom

Photography: Tony Miller

15

16

RUSHCUTTERS BAY APARTMENT   SYDNEY, NEW SOUTH WALES, AUSTRALIA   CHENCHOW LITTLE ARCHITECTS

The apartment is on the top floor of a new multi-unit residential building on the water at Rushcutters Bay. The building did not respond to its location or the user, providing a generic minimum standard dwelling with a tiny floor space. The client required the entire interior to be refitted (except the bathrooms). The challenge was to provide a contemporary interior which gave the illusion of more space, and which provided flexibility and storage.

Three main elements are used in this scheme: the white walls and cabinetry, which wrap around the periphery of the apartment; two dark timber volumes within the space, which contain the laundry and the kitchen; and the mirrored wall.

The three elements have very different qualities and have been strategically located to enhance the sense of space. The white walls wrap around the dark volumes, constantly leading the eye into the distance. The mirror, used at the point of greatest spatial restriction, enhances the sensation of space through reflection. Long continuous lines run through the apartment in the floor, ceiling, and walls to enhance the sense of space. The lines continue through different functional zones.

Continuous lines of aluminum extruded channels and white limestone run across the gray stone floor. Some house plumbing, electrical services and sliding door tracks; others are ornamental. Continuous lines in the ceiling house down-lights and sliding door tracks. The horizontal shelf running across the western wall moves through the kitchen, dining and lounge zones in the apartment.

The vertical lines on the western wall in the form of blade light columns, and the eastern wall in the form of recessed light shafts, provide continuity and structure to the main space, bridging the different ceiling heights and also enhancing the vertical. The blade light columns occur in the kitchen, dining and living spaces. The detailing system is continuous through each zone.

1   Hallway
2   Living (evening)

3

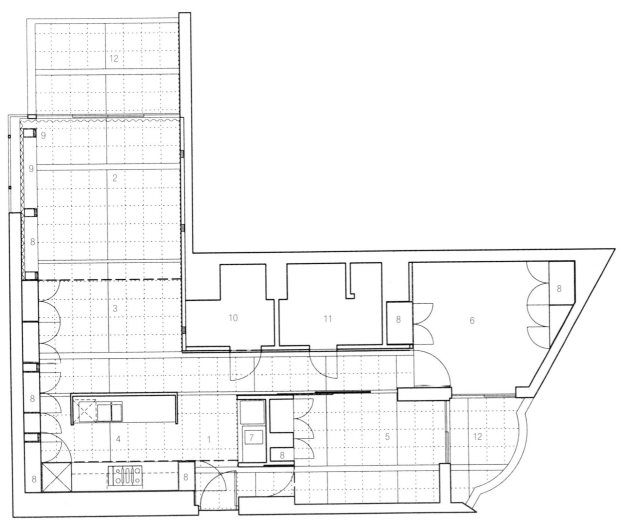

1   Entry
2   Living
3   Dining
4   Kitchen
5   Study/bedroom
6   Bedroom
7   Laundry
8   Storage
9   Bench seat
10 Guest ensuite
11 Bathroom
12 Balcony

4

5

6

3 Dining/living
4 Floor plan
5 Kitchen
6 Bookshelf detail
7 Living (day)

Photography: Bart Maiorana

7

SMART APARTMENT   SYDNEY, NEW SOUTH WALES, AUSTRALIA   SMART DESIGN STUDIO

This apartment in the heart of Kings Cross was transformed from an awkward studio into a one-bedroom apartment by the use of a sliding 'art wall' by Tim Richardson and the integration of a long joinery wall. The seamless meeting of art and architecture features throughout this project.

The design is strong and bold. A red lacquered joinery wall, like a very compact and functional Swiss Army knife, runs the full length of the apartment housing all the utilities; kitchen appliances, laundry, audiovisual equipment, wardrobe and general storage are hidden behind.

Red, chosen to reflect its location in Sydney's red-light district, gives this unit an identity, instead of simply a collection of cupboards and creates a clear distinction between old and new.

The original features, including window frames, ceilings, cornices, bathroom tiles and terrazzo flooring, of this handsome 1920s apartment block have been left intact. This contrast of old and new further adds to the visual impact of the space.

Although the apartment is only 40 square meters, the natural light from all sides and the cleanness of the design gives the impression of a far larger space. The flexibility of rooms further enhances this feeling of space. The custom-made bed doubles as a daybed, transforming an otherwise small bedroom into an extension of the living area.

Careful planning and detailing has achieved an apartment with a feeling of calmness instead of clutter and a mood that is unique and dynamic.

1   Red lacquer storage unit runs length of the apartment

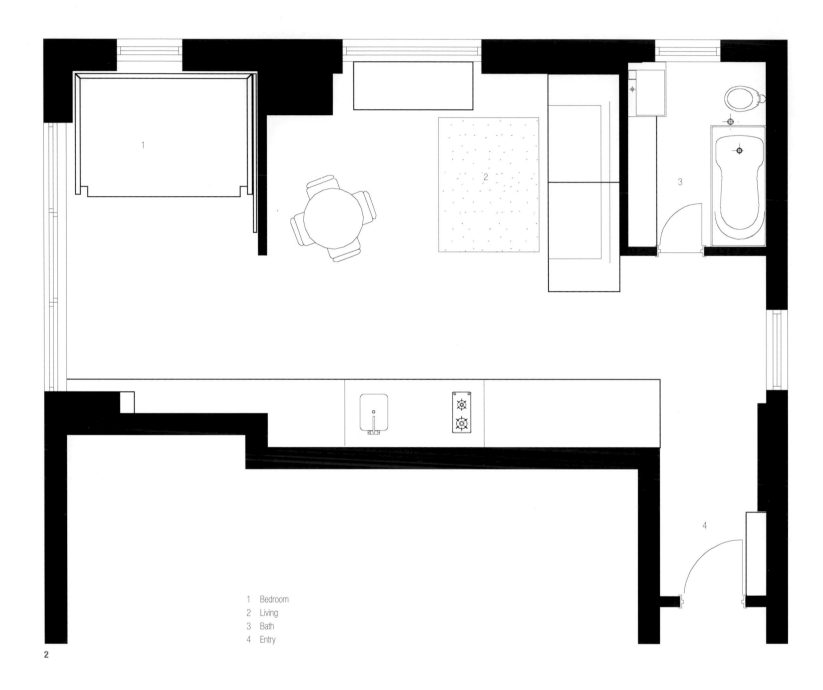

1 Bedroom
2 Living
3 Bath
4 Entry

3

4

5

6

2 Floor plan

3 Living/dining

4 Wall unit opens like a Swiss Army knife to reveal multiple functions

5 Flexibility of rooms enhances the feeling of space

6 Sliding doors imprint spells out DNA coding, creating a dynamic, functional piece of artwork

8

7 Black bean bed doubles as a daybed
8 Stainless steel bench top contrasts with original features of the bathroom
9 Screen by artist Tim Richards divides bedroom from living room

Photography: Sharrin Rees

9

SOHO LOFT   NEW YORK, NEW YORK, USA   AARDVARCHITECTURE

This 3000-square-foot loft renovation deals with the relationship between different scales of rooms—flexible, open spaces, and smaller private rooms. Both are set against a backdrop of 19th-century decorative detail and beyond, views to lower and mid-town Manhattan. The design juxtaposes the view framed by the windows to the interpenetrating spaces of the apartment's interior. As one moves through the spaces, shifting long and short views are offered. The framed images shift from frontal to oblique, and back.

The project was structured in phases to contain costs, with the architects contracting directly for all finishes to maintain high quality.

1   View from living area to entry foyer and kitchen, atelier at right

3

2   View from living room to photo studio
3   View from entry toward media room and living area
4   Dining and kitchen with antique Philippine work table

4

7

6

8

9 Master bathroom, view toward bedroom
10 Bedroom

Photography: Walter Mair, Zurich, Switzerland

9

10

SORRENTO   HONG KONG   STEVE LEUNG DESIGNERS LTD.

A streamlined, minimalist tranquility is achieved through contemporary and cosmopolitan styling, optimal spatial extension, and a relaxing atmosphere.

Simple, clean lines and a tone-on-tone color scheme on furniture and furnishings contribute to a sophisticated look for the 140-square-meter interior. Lights penetrate through the adjustable louver panels, inspiring the linear arrangement. Visual linkage between study and living room through the glass glazed walls helps to create the impression of space while maintaining individuality. The use of large windows on the side of the dining room creates a mirage for the apartment.

The use of different materials, such as sycamore wood and fabric, for walls and floorings, enhances the rich texture. Accompanied by deliberate mood lighting, the unique character is carried through to every corner of the apartment.

1   Large windows in dining room extend the space

1

2

3

4

5

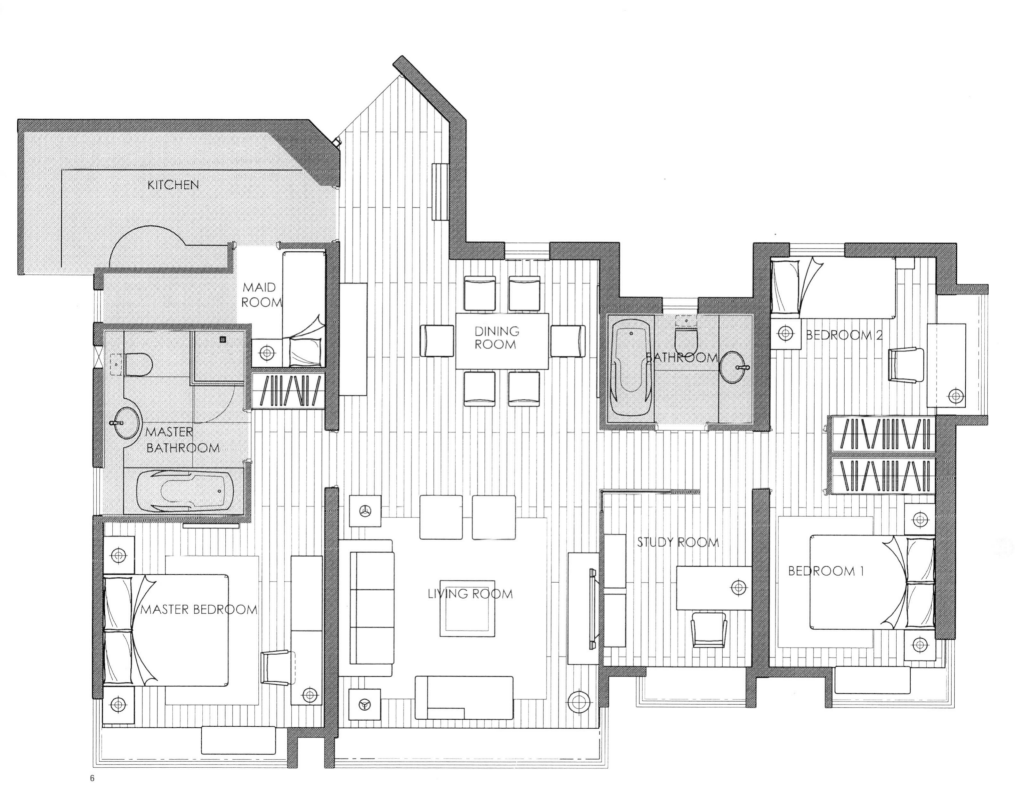

KITCHEN

MAID
ROOM

MASTER
BATHROOM

MASTER BEDROOM

DINING
ROOM

BATHROOM

LIVING ROOM

STUDY ROOM

BEDROOM 2

BEDROOM 1

6

7

8

9

7 Study area in bedroom 2
8 Study is adjacent to living room
9 Study
10 Bedroom 1 detail
11 Bedroom 1
12 Master bedroom has magnificent views

Photography: Ulso Tsang

10

11

12

STEEL LOFT   NEW YORK, NEW YORK, USA   GWATHMEY SIEGEL & ASSOCIATES ARCHITECTS

The goal with this apartment was to perceive the 'idea' of a single 4400-square-foot rectilinear volume, which is hierarchically modulated and articulated through the layering, horizontally and vertically, of the forms and space. The space, 110 feet long by 40 feet wide, has 14 (7 pairs) of south-facing windows on the seventh floor of a loft building in Chelsea.

A line of existing columns, 18 feet from the south façade, articulates the main circulation gallery. A second circulation zone, visual and actual, parallel to and along the south window wall, accesses more private spaces—study, master bedroom suite and master bath—through a sequence of thick wall niches that accommodate sliding steel and patterned glass doors for privacy.

The ceiling height to the underside of the slab is 9 foot 10 inches. Existing beams form a second ceiling layer and are the primary referential horizontal graphic through the entire space. Three ceiling/wall heights below the beams establish datums for primary and secondary walls, which do not engage the ceiling, but float below, exaggerating the illusion of a higher space. These varying ceiling heights afford opportunities to conceal ambient indirect lighting, as well as air-conditioning ducts and grilles, and preserve the overall spatial continuity. Major materials used include gray limestone, maple wood flooring, warm white walls, Anigre wood panels/cabinet, cold rolled steel, and stainless steel.

The loft is a three-dimensional reinterpretation of a Mondrian; it is an architecture that is at once articulate, graphic, sublime, and calm. It is a space conceived as an 'excavation,' a carving away that results in an essentialness that is inherently sculptural—light filled, dense and sequential, where nothing is added or redundant.

1 View from study

EINSTEIN'S
1912 MANUSCRIPT
ON THE
SPECIAL THEORY
OF RELATIVITY

1

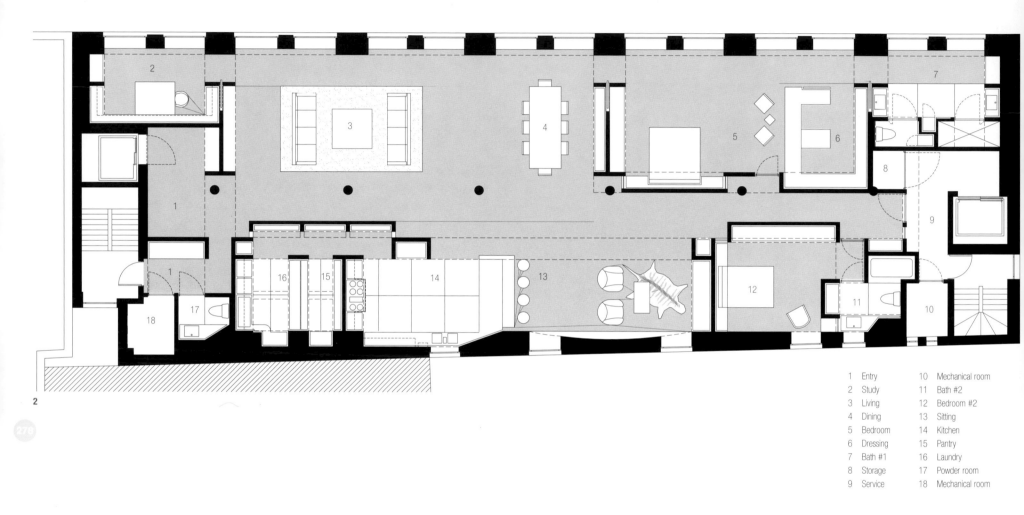

1	Entry	10	Mechanical room
2	Study	11	Bath #2
3	Living	12	Bedroom #2
4	Dining	13	Sitting
5	Bedroom	14	Kitchen
6	Dressing	15	Pantry
7	Bath #1	16	Laundry
8	Storage	17	Powder room
9	Service	18	Mechanical room

2   Floor plan

3   Living/dining view

4   Entry view

3

4

5

6

7

8

STUBBS ROAD APARTMENT   HONG KONG   BUILDING DESIGN STUDIO

A couple whose children had grown up and left home wanted to completely remodel the 175-square-meter family apartment to suit their lifestyle. The design developed in response to two apparently conflicting requirements. One client wanted an open plan design, the other preferred more cellular, private spaces. There are three main areas: the living room and wife's study make up the most open and public spaces; master bedroom, bathroom, husband's study and bathroom comprise the most private spaces; kitchen, utility and maids' rooms complete the apartment. The three areas are connected through a courtyard that doubles as the dining room and main entrance.

To achieve the conflicting requirements of openness and privacy, connections to the courtyard are by a series of large sliding panels and doors. Thus when desired, the apartment can achieve an open flow of spaces. Finishes were used to reinforce the idea of a courtyard: randomly patterned oak doors, outdoor tiles, backlit oak slats, and granite steps accommodating indoor landscaping.

In contrast to the courtyard, the other living areas have a more refined feel. In the living room, shades of blue and maple along with custom-designed tables by BDS are set off by the clients' artwork. The requirement to maximize storage space wherever possible is exemplified in the bed design. There were also two studies, both of which double as guest bedrooms. One study features an oversized mirror for practising golf swings, the other features a carpet designed by BDS.

Major materials used in the renovation include outdoor wall and floor tiles, and oak timber strips (courtyard); glass blocks, alta quartzite, and glass tiles (guest bath); woven timber panel, and maple timber floor (living room); lacewood veneer, artificial suede fabric, and wool carpet (master bedroom); and stainless steel (kitchen).

1   Entry/courtyard, with outdoor floor and wall tiles

2 Kitchen in stainless steel, white lacquer, grey terrazzo and black Corian
3 View from dining area toward study and indoor landscaping
4 Study featuring dimpled 'golf ball' wall behind television
5 Floor plan

2

3

4

1   Entry
2   Courtyard
3   Living room
4   Her study
5   Master bedroom
6   Master bathroom
7   His study
8   Guest bathroom
9   Kitchen
10 Maids' quarters/utility

6

6 Living room with custom-designed coffee and side tables

7 Living room with woven sycamore veneer panel cabinet for AV system

8 View of courtyard from study, with BDS-designed carpet

7

8

9

9   Master bedroom in soft brown suede, lacewood veneer and cream carpet
10 Milky glass blocks allow light to filter to internal bathroom
Photography: Frederick Wong

THE LOFT OF FRANK AND AMY   HELL'S KITCHEN, NEW YORK, USA   RESOLUTION: 4 ARCHITECTURE

Designed for an art critic and a film editor, the 4800-square-foot Loft of Frank and Amy is a
bare, wide-open play space in New York City's gritty Hell's Kitchen neighborhood. Located in
a former industrial building, the loft occupies an entire floor with full window exposure and
dynamic urban views on three sides. The design enhances this industrial context by posing
new construction as a single sculptural intervention within this existing space. This intervention
becomes a compressed box of utility (containing the kitchen, mechanical and supportive
spaces), that divides the public and private areas of the loft. A primary feature of the box
is a series of huge sliding doors that can open the entire perimeter of the loft, or conversely,
can extend to the exterior walls to close off the bedrooms.

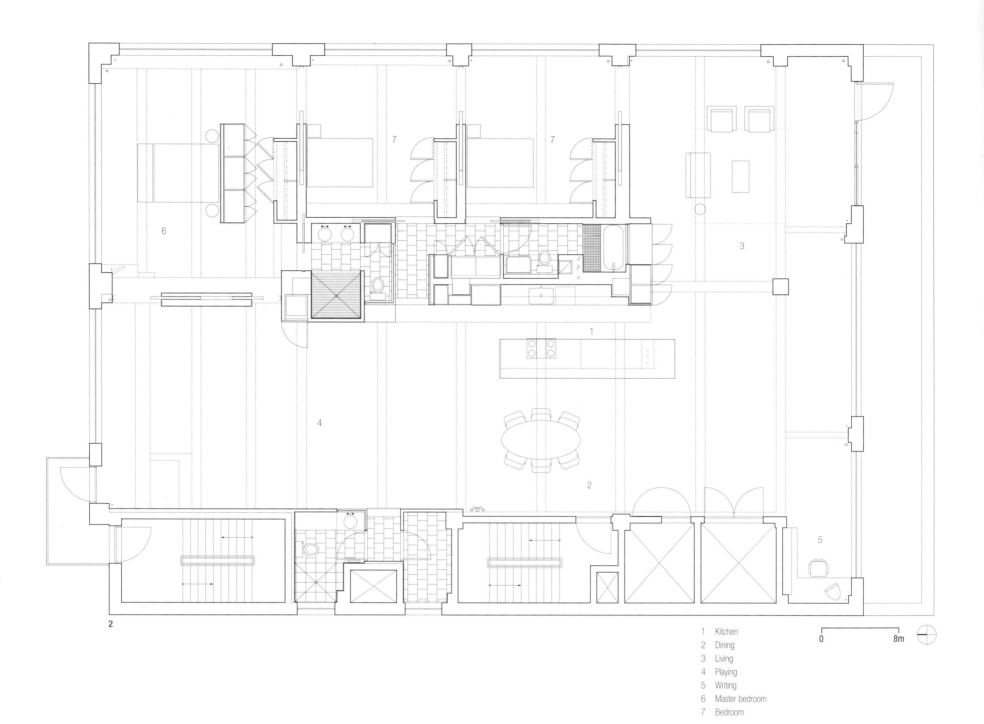

292

2

1	Kitchen
2	Dining
3	Living
4	Playing
5	Writing
6	Master bedroom
7	Bedroom

2 Floor plan
3 Kitchen
4 Dining and kitchen
5 Axonometric

3

4

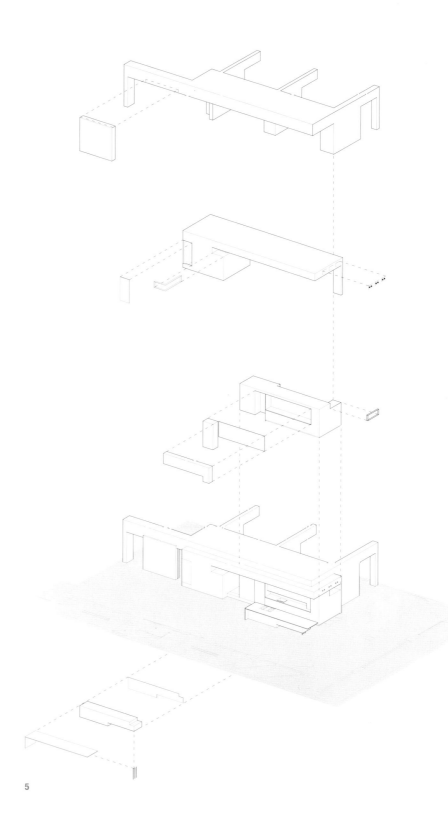

5

6

7

8

6 View of entry from 'utility box'
7 View of bathroom in the 'utility box'
8 Built-in cabinetry at master bedroom
9 Master bedroom

Photography: Paul Warchol

THE PEAK   JAKARTA, INDONESIA   PAI – PARAMITA ABIRAMA ISTASADHYA, PT

This 220-square-meter condominium is located in the central business district of Jakarta. Complete with service quarters, the apartment has three bedrooms, two with ensuite bathrooms, living, dining, study and pantry.

The interior design is energetic, with the use of contrasting dark woods, and the use of marble, solid and veneer mahogany, travertine, and glass. Soft furnishings are understated and of high quality. Window treatments are of natural silk, with a simple cut to enhance their natural beauty.

1   Study, with view to living room

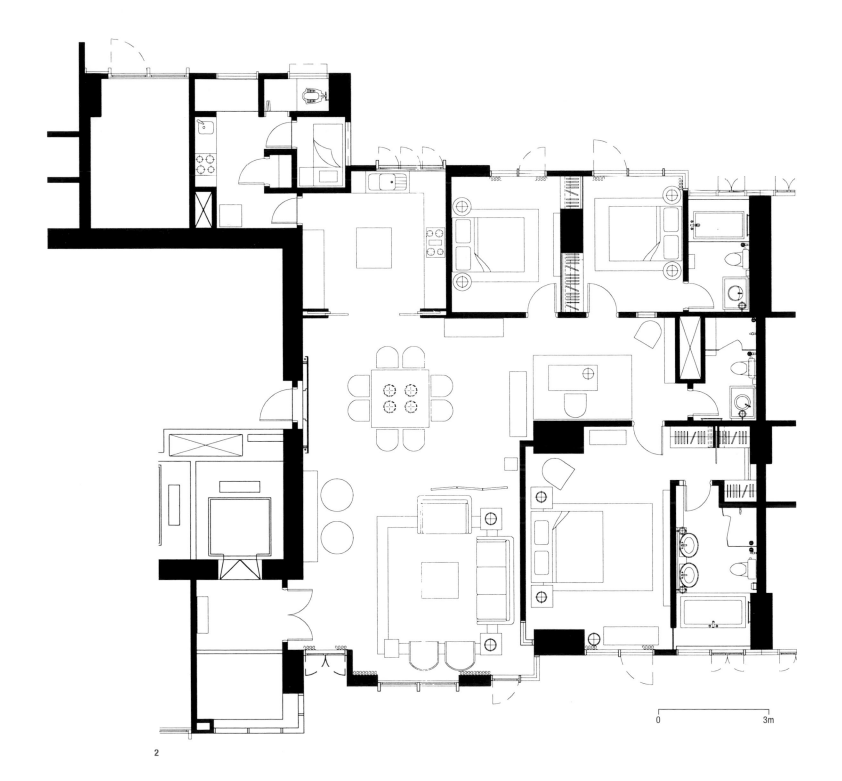

0   3m

2 Floor plan
3 Dining room with view to study
4 Kitchen, glass panel doors retracted

4

3

5

Photography: Oki Sutrisno

6

7

8

THE UPPER EAST SHANGHAI, CHINA STEVE LEUNG DESIGNERS LTD.

A strong contrasting theme of black and white throughout this 120-square-meter apartment signifies the distinctive character of cold winter, yet a little lime green neutralizes the chilly feel, creating an incredible harmony to a homey environment.

Optimizing the living room's space and vision, a study is located adjacent, separated by a half-wall-height cabinet, extending the living room while maintaining a private space for work and study. Opaque glass walls subtly crystallize the views and help highlight the surroundings, in the alternate adoption of white matte-painted walls.

Custom-made furniture with sharp outlines and stainless steel accents adds frosty feelings to match the furnishings. A characteristic tree artwork in the dining room not only coheres ideally with the winter ambience, but also adds extra sense of humor by its reversed echo in the master bedroom, extending the passionate black and white contrast to the utmost!

1 Dining room
2 Living room
3 Living room detail with contrast color accent

1

3

2

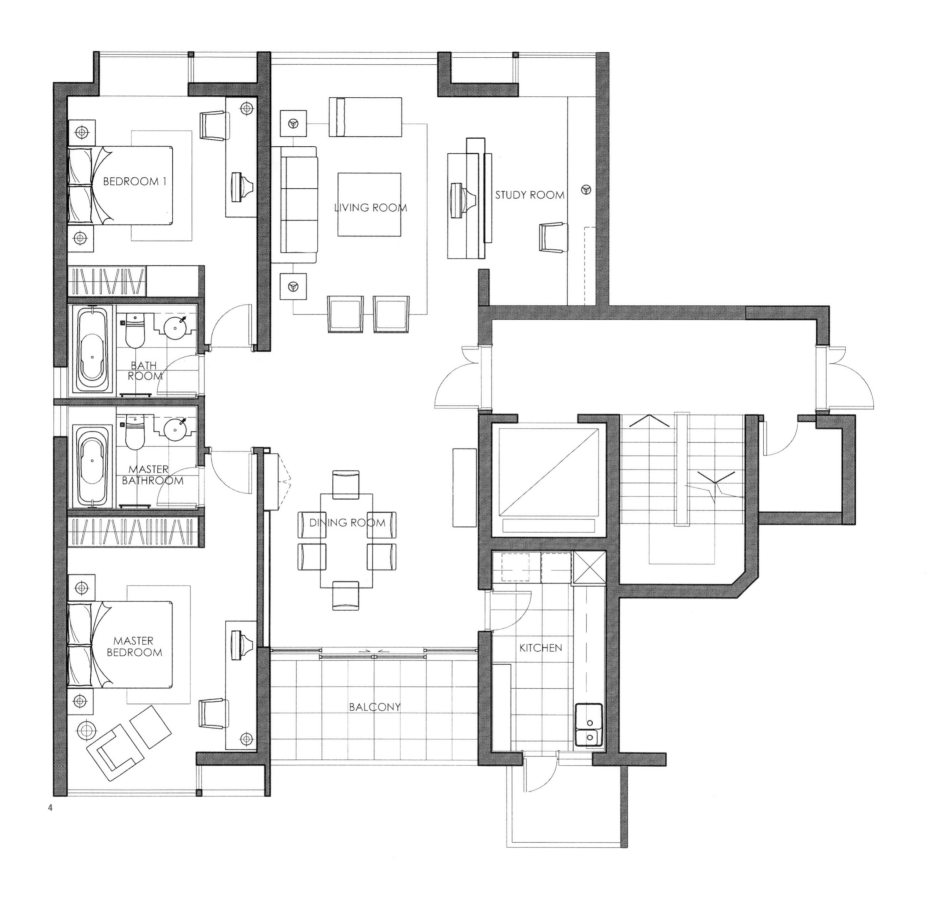

BEDROOM 1

LIVING ROOM

STUDY ROOM

BATH ROOM

MASTER BATHROOM

DINING ROOM

MASTER BEDROOM

KITCHEN

BALCONY

4

5

6

7

9

10

Photography: Ulso Tsang

VANCOUVER RESIDENCE   VANCOUVER, BRITISH COLUMBIA, CANADA   MITCHELL FREEDLAND DESIGN

The inspiration for the complete renovation of this 3800-square-foot penthouse apartment came from the client's many years of living in Japan.

The client, a single businessman, was relocating back to North America from Japan. He was looking for large open spaces as a backdrop for his collection of Asian contemporary art and antique collectables. The environment was to incorporate traditional Japanese and Frank Lloyd Wright aesthetics translated into a spare modern vocabulary.

The penthouse has magnificent views. The client's desire was to open up the plan as much as possible, while retaining a private bed and bath retreat. The difficulty of working within the existing plumbing and structural restraints influenced the design triumphs of the project. The glassed-in powder room was initiated by the plumbing's existing location and the narrow space it was located in. This led to the development of a series of wood-clad archways within which the glass box was set. This progression created a wondrous arrival corridor for the residence. The desire to have a central fireplace in the living room instigated the creation of the large display/storage unit. The monolithic element anchors the vast living and dining space, as well as providing a passage to the kitchen from the entry hall.

Once again, the existing plumbing location in the master bedroom was the 'given' that other elements were planned around. Limestone, mahogany, slate and glass were used to adorn the architectural elements within this bath space.

The simple, unadorned use of cherrywood, mahogany, slate, glass and steel are the unifying elements that reinforce the overall Japanese aesthetic desired by the client. Contemporary and classic modern furniture harmoniously coexists within the clean and airy environment created. Custom-designed lighting systems enhance the overall architectural effect.

2

3

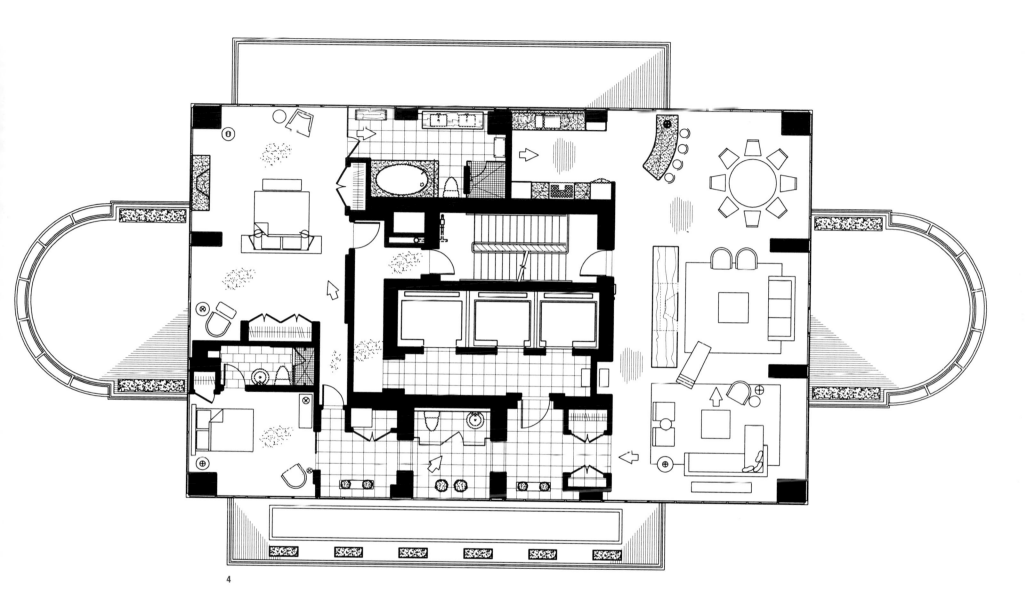

4

2 Front entry corridor and glass-enclosed powder room
3 Master bathroom
4 Floor plan

6

7

5 Powder room

6 Living room

7 Kitchen, dining room and night view beyond

Photography: Ed White Photographics

VILLA DEL ROSE   SINGAPORE   SCDA ARCHITECTS

Reductive is the word that comes to mind to describe the clean, quiet tones in this refurbished two-level, 2000-square-foot apartment in an old maisonette block near the Botanical Gardens.

The apartment is a longitudinal shaped plan leading to a full-length balcony that opens out to a tree-filled view. SCDA's renovation of the apartment involved a number of structural changes—angles were straightened, a wall on the upper level was repositioned, and a storeroom on the lower level was omitted, but the main functional areas were left intact.

Plain-faced cabinetry of light timber elegantly demarcates the living and dining areas as well as providing storage and display. These fixtures imbue the spaces with a coherent, architectural character. The surfaces are kept uniformly 'clean'—even the light fittings, including those in the bathrooms, are all recessed, to de-emphasize the fixtures.

A 'wood-wall' in the dining room replaces an aluminum-framed frosted glass window that looks over the air-well. This plain-faced fixture is a unifying element in the overall reductive scheme. Daylight still enters but through two narrow vertical openings on the wood-wall, resulting in the dining room taking on a more sequestered character. In keeping with the architect's intention of 'clarifying the space', existing structures are re-expressed, particularly the staircase and balcony. The staircase is reduced to just the timber treads, cantilevered into a specially thickened wall. The banister, a basic metal frame, has been retained for safety purposes.

Water, a hallmark of SCDA's architecture, has been used in this project to enhance the design. The balcony becomes a reflection pool when filled with water, enhancing the owners' enjoyment of the greenery just outside.

Upper level

Lower level

6

4 Transparent staircase, reduced to its timber treads
5 Balcony is transformed into a reflection pool
6 View from hallway, looking into master bath

5

7   Bathroom on lower level

8   Honed beige limestone lines interior of bath

Photography: Peter Mealin/SCDA Architects

7

8

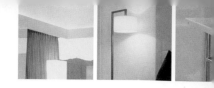

YEUNG APARTMENT   HONG KONG   DWP CL3

The 186-square-meter area was divided into practical spaces: a living/dining room, kitchen, study/guestroom and three bedrooms. The stunning views of Victoria Harbour from the living room dictated that nothing could obstruct the view. Instead of ceiling lights, which would cause unnecessary glare at night, a hidden trough was created and custom-made lighting was installed, washing the upper walls with a soft glow. To create the trough, a false inner wall was required that would end short of the ceiling. To minimize the amount of living space lost, the false wall was tapered so that that it slants toward the floor. This angled wall also functions as a partition between the living area and the private space.

The space is subtle and neutral in palette but not devoid of texture. Finishes include a near-seamless floor laid from rectangular sandstone tiles, vertical planes of glass which clad the living room and champagne-tinted aluminum which surrounds the dining area and is also used in the housing for the wide-screen television. A contrasting blast of strong color is introduced through the vermilion acrylic canvases by Malaysian artist Kumari Nahappan, which pepper the space.

Opposite
Built-in TV unit and view from living area

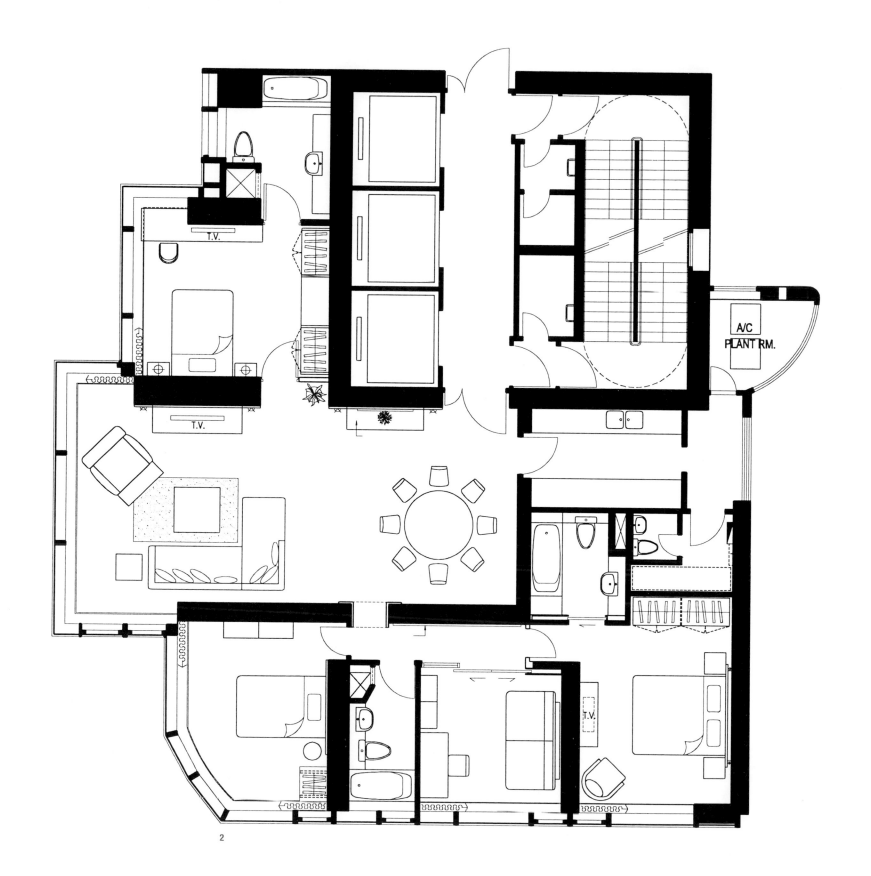

T.V.

T.V.

A/C
PLANT RM.

T.V.

2

3

4

5

2 Floor plan
3 Dining area through to living area
4 Living area detail
5 Guest bathroom
6 Bedroom

Photography: Wu Kin Yat

6

ZIGGURAT 8.2, PENTHOUSE APARTMENT
CLERKENWELL, LONDON, UK FORM DESIGN ARCHITECTURE

The awkward configuration of the existing shell space ultimately proved to be a positive generator for the design of this 2200-square-foot penthouse apartment.

A fluid series of distinct sub-spaces—defined by mood, function, volume, and outlook—have been created within an essentially open plan. A mezzanine floor inserted over the central wing of the plan provides the owner's gallery bedroom and bathroom as well as access, via a glazed slot, to an upper-level roof terrace.

A highly formalized double-height sitting area is counter-balanced by the more enclosed dining and sitting spaces accommodated under the central mezzanine. The horizon view to the north from this latter space is accentuated by its linear geometry and the rising curved profile of the soffit. With north, east and west outlooks, there is an ever-changing play of natural light within the space.

Within the formal sitting area, a double-height Mondrian-inspired grid of panels opens like an advent calendar to reveal media, emergency exit, storage and bar. The largest panel, in fact a wardrobe block accessed from its reverse face, slides electrically to enclose the gallery bedroom.

On the upper level, the master bedroom has specially designed storage for shirts and shoes and a television that rises up from a cupboard opposite the bed. Across the top-lit glazed hall, which also provides access to some 1200 square feet of external terraces, is the master bathroom which incorporates a walk-in shower, over which are two large shower heads purpose-designed by the practice, which feature fiber optics to bathe the occupant in light as well as water.

1 View from main double-height living area to kitchen and gallery bedroom
2 Library and dining areas

1   Common lobby
2   Entrance hall
3   Sitting (double height)
4   Kitchen
5   Dining
6   Sitting (curved ceiling)
7   Study
8   Guest bedroom
9   Guest bathroom
10 Utility
11 W.C.
12 Terrace
13 Bedroom
14 Bathroom
a   Media wall
b   Fireplace
c   Rolling wardrobe
d   Roof light over
e   Shower
f   Wild grass planter
g   Pool

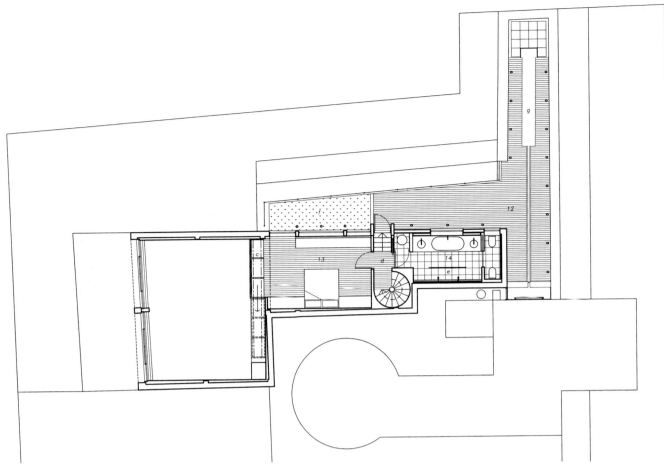

3

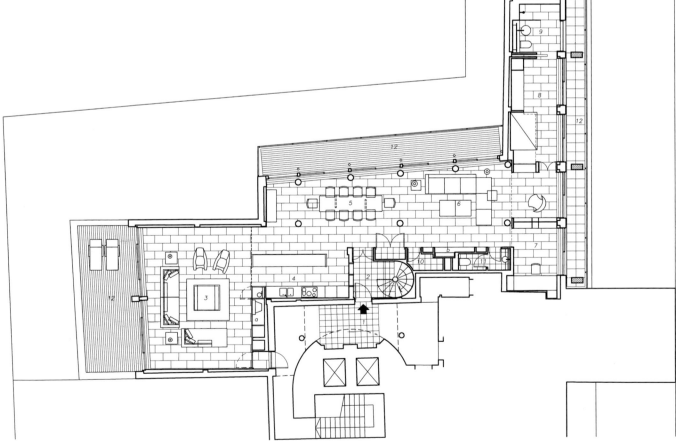

4

0   3m

5

6

3 Upper floor plan
4 Lower floor plan
5 Library and dining areas showing contemporary fireplace
6 Double-height living room and terrace
7 Master bathroom, where shower bathes the occupant in light and water
8 Double-height living room from gallery bedroom
9 Gallery bedroom with views across city

Photography: Jeremy Lingard, Form Design Architecture (5,6,8); Matthew Weinreb (1,2,7,9)

7

8

9

INDEX OF ARCHITECTS

SEATTLE

JAKARTA

SÃO PAULO

SYDNEY

LONDON

VANCOUVER

SHANGHAI

HONG KONG